# The National Maritime Museum

Edited by Dr. Basil Greenhill C.B., C.M.G.

Scala/Philip Wilson

First published in 1982 by
Philip Wilson Publishers Ltd and Summerfield Press Ltd
Russell Chambers, Covent Garden, London WC2E 8AA

Photography by Angelo Hornak and
Scala Istituto Fotografico Editoriale
Designed by Peter Ling
Edited by Philip Wilson Publishers Ltd, London
Series Editor: Judy Spours

Produced by Scala Istituto Fotografico Editoriale, Firenze
Phototypeset by Tradespools Ltd, Frome, Somerset
Printed in Italy

ISBN 0 85667 133 9

**Acknowledgements**
The authors and publishers would like to acknowledge the use
of illustrations of the following objects:
lodestone, p.95; ivory presentation set of navigation instruments, p.97; octant by George Adams and backstaff by W. K.
Garner, p.98; telescope by Jacob Cunigham, p.101; telescope
by Frazer & Son, p.101; theodolite by H. Cole and graphometer by P. Danfrie, p.96; theodolite by Sisson, p.102; and
barometer by I. Patrick, p.102 from the Sir James Caird
Collection;
Haiti logboat, p.38 on loan from R. W. Warwick.

*Copies of all illustrations in this book may be obtained from the
National Maritime Museum, whose own transparencies are
marked* (NMM) *after the caption of the illustration.*

*Front cover: Battle of the Glorious First of June 1794* by Philip de
Loutherbourg, oil on canvas, 1795

*Back cover:* Seaman's crafts (see p. 139)

# Contents

# Foreword

BASIL GREENHILL
*Director*

The National Maritime Museum traces its history back to the eighteenth century and before, but it is only in recent years that it has developed into the leading institution of its kind in the world. It is unique in its role as a very large general historical museum concentrating on the maritime aspects of the development of human culture and technology.

The Museum covers many fields, and its collections are comprehensive and its organization very complex. In this book, some of the Heads of Department and members of the senior curatorial staff themselves explain the work of the Museum for which they are responsible. The contributions were written independently and lead on naturally one from the other. All express, either directly or by inference, the deep satisfaction in their work derived by the staff of such an institution as the National Maritime Museum.

The contributions also reveal some of the problems of the workings of a big museum in the modern world. The demands placed on museums are both much wider and more complicated than they used to be, and are always increasing. Standards of scholarship must still be maintained against all pressures, yet at the same time we must communicate effectively in the galleries with a growing number of visitors, many of them unfamiliar with the material they come to see. Standards of conservation are steadily rising, and we attach great importance to their further improvement at Greenwich. So the classic tensions between curator, designer, and conservator, administrator and scholar, between the display itself and the proper interpretation and conservation of the material, do not diminish.

At the National Maritime Museum we feel we have been fortunate in being able to minimize these difficulties, thanks to the mutual cooperation of a staff highly skilled in their various functions. In this book some of them present the story in their own words.

The **Silver Jubilee Sundial**, designed by Christopher St J. H. Daniel (Museum staff) and executed in bronze by the sculptor Edwin Russell, takes the form of two dolphins on the crest of a wave, holding the dial plate in their jaws. The gap between the shadows of their tails indicates the time to within a minute. The dial stands in a garden to the south of the Main Buildings of the Museum and forms a theoretical link with the Old Royal Observatory.

**The Main Buildings** of the National Maritime Museum. The Queen's House stands in the centre of the picture; beyond, the Royal Naval College and the River Thames. ▷

# Introduction

C. St. J. H. DANIEL
*Head of the Department of Museum Services*

*'Earth has not anything to show more fair:*
*Dull would he be of soul who could pass by*
*A sight so touching in its majesty:'*

Sonnet – Composed upon Westminster Bridge, 3 September 1802
WILLIAM WORDSWORTH 1770–1850

Looking towards London across the Royal Park of Greenwich, from the promontory on which General Wolfe's statue stands or from some vantage point such as Vanbrugh Castle, the view can be breathtaking. Even on a dull wet day it calls for a second glance, but on a fine summer's morning or on a misty autumnal afternoon, you can stretch your eyes and drink in the scene.

In the distance lies the great city: in the foreground are the green vistas and gentle slopes of the Park, the forest trees and the magnificent buildings of the National Maritime Museum. Momentarily we can recapture the past, as we glimpse the river and gaze at the view, which surely must have made every bygone traveller on the Dover road pause on reaching the crest of the hill. Wordsworth might just as easily have composed his famous sonnet here, except for its last line, 'And all that mighty heart is lying still!' Nothing could be further from the truth.

The National Maritime Museum is a highly dynamic museum and this book, written by its staff, does not simply describe the collections but explains something of the workings, revealing the hive of activity and industry that makes this the largest and finest institution of its kind anywhere in the world.

**The Old Royal Observatory** seen through the trees of 'one tree hill' in Greenwich Park. The Observatory is an integral part of the National Maritime Museum.

Set in the beautiful rural surroundings of Greenwich Park, the Museum primarily occupies two groups of buildings: the Main Buildings which are centred round the Queen's House, and the Old Royal Observatory on the hill to the south overlooking the River Thames. With justification, it has been described as the most beautiful museum in Britain. It is, of course, a great maritime museum in every sense, but it is also an important art gallery and the principal museum of the history of navigation and astronomy in the world. It is also an archival repository, an international centre for historical research, an educational establishment and an outstanding national architectural treasure, as well as a leading authority on conservation techniques and the parent museum for a number of outstations, including the Royal Research Ship *Discovery*.

The Museum is primarily concerned with the history of most aspects of man's encounter with the sea. This includes not only the history of the Royal Navy but that of the whole shipping industry, set against the background of social, economic and technical change. The history of astronomy, of time-determination and measurement, of navigation and hydrography, are also major themes which are all part of this same encounter. Each theme is illustrated with extensive and informative displays, imaginatively designed and set out in fine modern galleries. Each display tells its own story and has been carefully planned not only to show the best the Museum has to offer but also to excite the interest of the visitor. The visitor who is unfamiliar with the National Maritime Museum might be doubtful of the suggestion that there is 'something for everyone', but the visitor who is familiar with the Museum will know the truth of this statement.

In New Neptune Hall there is a full-sized steamship, the paddle-tug *Reliant*; in the Barge House there are the glittering royal state barges of the seventeenth and eighteenth centuries; and only a few paces away, you can

△ **The steam paddle-tug *Reliant*** (156 gross tons) in New Neptune Hall. Once a coal-burner, her engines and her port paddle-wheel are now driven electrically. She has two independent side-lever, surface condensing, disconnecting paddle engines totalling 400 i.h.p. which gave her a maximum speed of 11 knots.

△ **Stern-view of the *Reliant*** in a splendid centre-piece of a display illustrating the history of steam powered ship development. The overall length of the *Reliant* is 106 ft 6 in.

**The Barge House.** A head-on view of Prince Frederick's Barge of    ▷
1732, designed by William Kent.

**Mythological ceiling painting** in the Great Hall of the Queen's House. The Great hall is a 40 ft cube. This magnificent painting, which dominates the ceiling, is attributed to Sir James Thornhill (1675–1734) whose greatest achievement was the famous Painted Hall in the Royal Naval College.

masterpieces of different periods in maritime history, depicting the smoke of battle as well as the peacable sight of merchant vessels under sail. The collections of silver, porcelain and glass, uniforms, swords and medals all relate to the daily life and activity associated with ships and the sea. Exquisitely constructed models show dockyards from Roman times to the present, and there are huge replicas of the great luxury liners of the twentieth century. All this (and much more) means that a day at the Museum is merely likely to whet the appetite. And if your aim is serious research there are an excellent library, extensive archives, a large collection of prints and historic photographs and considerable reserve collections, together with the resources and expertise of the specialists in many fields at work in the Museum.

### History of the Museum

Although it traces its origins back to the Royal Naval Museum in Somerset House in the eighteenth century, to the picture collection of King Charles I and to the institution of the Royal Observatory by Charles II in 1675, the National Maritime Museum is one of the youngest of the great national museums. It was formally established by an Act of Parliament in 1934, which authorised the illustration and study of the maritime history of Great Britain. This, though, was the culmination of many years of preparatory work and the immense

find yourself in a full-scale reconstruction of an archaeological rescue dig in the Kent marshes, the black mud almost oozing underfoot. There is the elegance and splendour of the Queen's House, evocative of royal life in another age. There are beautiful paintings, eloquent

**The Claude Jacobs collection** of engraved glass, dating mostly from the late eighteenth to the early nineteenth century. Jacobs (1890–1972) was a shipowner with a love of the sea, who, for over fifty years, sought and acquired fine glasses which had been decorated with ships and seamen.

A model of a medieval port *c* 1480, part of a series of beautifully constructed dioramas in Gallery 11, beneath the bow of the *Reliant*. These models illustrate shipbuilding in iron and steel, and cargo-handling through the ages.

**The Denny Shipyard** at Dumbarton, Scotland, the birth-place of many railway steamers and small naval craft. One of the intricately detailed models in Gallery 11.

**RMS *Windsor Castle*.** A superb model of the Union Castle passenger liner (37,640 gross tons), one of a trio of ship models, all built to the same scale, forming the centre-piece of the Living at Sea 1845–1975 display in Gallery 15. She carried 881 passengers and 475 crew.

A first class cabin from the Canadian Pacific trans-Atlantic passenger liner of the 1950s, *Empress of Canada* (New Neptune Hall).

9

**Bust of Sir James Caird** (1864–1954), 1st Baronet of Glenfarquhar, the Museum's most notable benefactor, at the entrance to the magnificent library which bears his name.

generosity of many benefactors. Most notable of these was Sir James Caird (1864–1954), 1st Baronet of Glenfarquhar, a Scottish ship owner who devoted much of his life and most of his fortune to the preservation of important maritime and scientific historical material. He would purchase not only individual items but entire collections – paintings, drawings, books, atlases, manuscripts, ship models and scientific instruments. Indeed, it is said that the great sale-rooms held auctions for his benefit alone. It is probably true to say that the Museum in its present form owes its very existence to Sir James Caird. Almost every department of the Museum is indebted to him, especially the library and manuscript sections, and if the donations of books and manuscript material were not enough, he also defrayed the costs of converting various buildings for Museum purposes, including the construction of the great library which now bears his name and the architecture of the grounds.

An appeal for funds was launched in 1921, and in 1926, when official Government recognition was given to the scheme for a national maritime museum, a Board of Trustees was set up under the chairmanship of the 7th Earl Stanhope. This body organized the purchase or acquisition of various collections, including the Macpherson Collection of maritime paintings, prints, drawings and atlases, the Greenwich Hospital Collection of pictures and the collections of the Royal Naval College. At about the same time, the Royal Hospital School, Greenwich moved to new premises in Holbrook in Suffolk, and it was decided by the Board of Admiralty that the vacated buildings would serve as a suitable home for the new maritime museum. By the time the Act of Parliament officially established the Museum, many important collections had been assembled.

The first Director was the distinguished naval historian Sir Geoffrey Callendar, who also played a large part in establishing the museum along with Sir James Caird and others. The skeleton of the Museum is basically the same today as it was then, except for the enormous expansion and changes that have taken place in the intervening years.

The Museum was officially opened on 27 April 1937, by His Majesty King George VI. On that royal occasion the King, accompanied by Queen Elizabeth, Queen Mary, Princess Elizabeth and Princess Margaret Rose, delivered an address to an assembled gathering of some 1600 guests in what is now called New Neptune Hall, and declared the Museum open. At that time there were no more than a dozen exhibition galleries, including the Queen's House and part of the West Wing, a reading room and accommodation for offices, workshop, restaurant and store rooms.

The Museum was closed to the public in the years 1939–46 and most of the exhibits were dispersed for safe-keeping, some to Somerset and some to Hampshire. Meanwhile, the Admiralty occupied the East and West Wings, while for a time in 1943–4 the WRNS used the Queen's House. Despite the disruption caused by the War years, from 1946 until 1967 under the second Director, Frank G. G. Carr, the Museum grew slowly and steadily. In 1968 Basil Greenhill joined the Museum as Director and began a programme of modernization and development which changed the former character of the Museum almost beyond recognition, and which made it the great institution it is today. Now, with a staff of over 400 people and facilities unimaginable only a few years ago, the National Maritime Museum is an example of a museum which has kept pace with changing times and the changing demands of society and one which will no doubt continue to do so.

# The Buildings

P. G. W. ANNIS
*Deputy Director*

Before any of the present buildings which make up the National Maritime Museum were begun, the Manor of Greenwich, created by Henry V after Agincourt (1415) and subsequently passed to his brother Humphrey, Duke of Gloucester, belonged to the Crown. The biggest group of buildings is situated at the northern edge of Greenwich Park and today comprises the Museum Main Buildings and the Royal Naval College. To the south, at the top of the hill in the Park, stands the second group of buildings now known as the Old Royal Observatory, which was founded by Charles II on 22 June 1675.

The story of all these buildings begins in 1427 when Humphrey of Gloucester erected a tower on the site now occupied by the Old Royal Observatory as a defence against possible invasion. Later he acquired some 200 acres of land on the south bank of the River Thames and there, close to the river, built his palace of Bella Court. It was Margaret of Anjou, wife of Henry VI, who proceeded to develop the palace into the Palace of Pleasance or Placentia.

The building was extended by successive monarchs, including Edward IV, Richard III, Henry VII and later Henry VIII, who was born there. All that remains of the Palace of Placentia today is the Crypt, a cellar in the Queen Anne Block of the Royal Naval College.

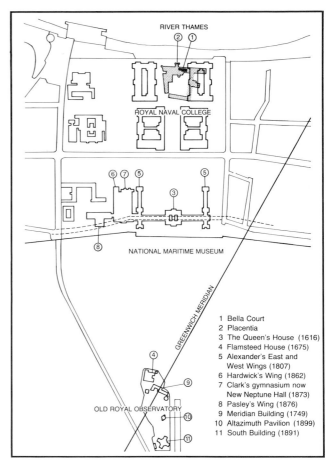

1 Bella Court
2 Placentia
3 The Queen's House (1616)
4 Flamsteed House (1675)
5 Alexander's East and West Wings (1807)
6 Hardwick's Wing (1862)
7 Clark's gymnasium now New Neptune Hall (1873)
8 Pasley's Wing (1876)
9 Meridian Building (1749)
10 Altazimuth Pavilion (1899)
11 South Building (1891)

The Main Buildings at the northern edge of Greenwich Park; the Queen's House and Alexander's two wings.

The site and its development.

Duke Humphrey's Tower and the Palace of Placentia, with London to the north-west. A view from Greenwich Park by an unknown artist, c 1620 (NMM CT B2854)

In 1613 James I settled Greenwich Park on his wife, Anne of Denmark, and three years later she was in consultation with the King's Surveyor, Inigo Jones (1573–1652), concerning a new house situated south of Placentia but still within James's recently enclosed Park. This new building, called 'House of Delights' or 'Queen's House', was in fact designed by Inigo Jones as an architectural link between the gardens of Placentia and the Park. The plan was H-shaped, and formed a bridge over the Deptford–Woolwich road which Humphrey of Gloucester had left as a public thoroughfare when he obtained the land nearly 200 years before. Unhappily, Anne died three years after the work began, the building was incomplete and James lost interest in the project. The Manor of Greenwich passed to Charles, Prince of

The Queen's House from the south-east.

Wales, who retained it on his accession as Charles I in 1625.

The building and decoration of the Queen's House were completed by 1635 and Queen Henrietta Maria, wife of Charles I, became the first owner. No expense was spared in the decoration of the Queen's House; tapestries, wall paintings, furniture and an abundance of statues made an interior which could fairly match the splendours of Venice. The Venetian style of the design, stemming from the architects Palladio and Scamozzi, whom Inigo Jones had met on his Italian travels, was later enriched by the works of Flemish Baroque artists, but the principal ornament of the house was the colourful and ornately framed ceiling painting in the Great Hall. Here a series of decorations by Orazio Gentileschi provided a classically disciplined yet delightful arrangement of allegorical scenes, a feature introduced directly from Italy.

Today, the most richly decorated of the rooms is the Queen's Bedroom. The painted frieze in this room is all that remains of the many original decorations. The central ceiling decoration was added when the earlier painting was removed. It is believed that the present central decoration in the Great Hall was the work of Sir James Thornhill's pupils. It was added comparatively recently and came from Halnaker House near Chichester.

The period of the Civil War (1642–9) saw extensive damage to Placentia but relatively little to the Queen's House, and after the Restoration Henrietta Maria returned to reside there for a short time. In 1661–2 two further Bridge Rooms were added to the east and west of the existing one. These additional apartments, making the plan a square, were built for her by John Webb

(1611–72), the nephew and pupil of Inigo Jones. Alterations and additions continued as the House passed into the ownership of Catherine of Braganza, wife of Charles II, and then to Mary of Modena, wife of James II. Two years after the 'Glorious Revolution' of 1688, the *coup* in which James was deposed and replaced by his daughter Mary and her husband William III, Charles Sackville, Earl of Dorset, was appointed Ranger of the Park and the Queen's House became the Ranger's residence. Apart from brief occupation by Caroline of Brandenburg–Ansbach, wife of George II, henceforth the building was not used by the Royal Family.

It was Charles II who conceived the idea of building a King's House on the site of the declined Palace of Placentia and John Webb was appointed the architect responsible for the creation of what is now the east part of the King Charles Block of the Royal Naval College. By March 1663 the ground plan and foundations had been made in the Queen's House garden and by January 1664 the foundations of the new Palace had been laid according to Webb's designs. But, alas, Charles II ran out of money and the project was abandoned, leaving the site available for development for another purpose.

△ The Great Hall of the Queen's House today, looking towards the south.

The Queen's bedroom in the Queen's House; a detail of the ceiling decoration.

The main purpose was, ostensibly at least, a charitable one. The general idea, held by James II, was that retired seamen should be treated in much the same way as his elder brother had treated retired soldiers at the Royal Hospital at Chelsea. James's daughter, Mary II, pursued her father's ideas and the Royal Hospital at Greenwich was founded by a Charter of William and Mary dated 25 October 1694. However, it was not until March 1695 that a Commission was set up to put 'The said good and pious purpose into existence'. Sir Christopher Wren (1632–1723) as Surveyor General was chosen as architect of the new buildings, but his original plan of 1694 was to include a dome on the Queen's House and was rejected. In another plan of 1697, six blocks connected by colonnades to the Queen's House were reduced to two blocks and Wren always complained that the Queen's House was too small to incorporate into a grand design. However, the final plan with the twin domes forms the basis of a wooden model of the Hospital, now in the National Maritime Museum, which, it is believed, was constructed in 1699 by Hawksmoor from Wren's design.

Nicholas Hawksmoor (1661–1736), who became Assistant Surveyor in 1705, was the guiding hand behind the King William Block that was finished in 1708. Working in close sympathy with Sir John Vanbrugh (1664–1726), who became Comptroller of Works in 1703, the Queen Anne Block was largely finished by them in 1705, although the final details were added in 1731 by Hawksmoor's successor Colin Campbell.

The Painted Hall was decorated by Sir James Thornhill and much of its interior was designed by Hawksmoor. It took Thornhill, with the help of assistants, twenty years to complete the decoration, but despite the inevitable changes in style they achieved a pictorial and architectural unity which is to be found nowhere else in English art.

Henry Sidney, Earl of Romney, became Ranger of Greenwich Park in 1697 and in 1699 diverted the road which ran under the bridges of the Queen's House to the north, and so the original concept of a link between Palace and Park disappeared. From then on the buildings north of the road had their own life as Hospital and later Naval College. The buildings to the south, Queen's House and Observatory, have a different history.

Romney remained Ranger until 1708 when he was bought out by Prince George of Denmark, husband of Queen Anne, who obtained the services of the Commissioners of Greenwich Hospital in carrying out repairs. Though the Queen's House was empty, Wren and Vanbrugh were architects in charge and Hawksmoor was Clerk of Works. The Commissioners of the King's Works resumed responsibility in George II's reign when

◁ The north face of the Queen's House and Flamsteed House on its hill. The new dome of the Great, or South East, Equatorial Building is to the left of Flamsteed House.

The south front of the Queen's House.

The Observatory, Queen's House and King's House with the remains of Placentia. A view from Greenwich Park, attributed to J. Vorstermans, c 1680. (NMM CT A9004)

his wife occupied the building. Some time after Queen Caroline's death, Lady Catherine Pelham lived there (from 1743 to 1780) but the House remained mostly empty until the Princess Caroline of Wales, who became Ranger in 1796, sold it to the Commissioners of the Royal Naval Asylum in 1806 when that body transferred to Greenwich.

At first the children of the Royal Naval Asylum, which educated the sons and daughters of naval ratings, lived in the 'Ranger's House' as the Queen's House had become known, but as it was inadequate for their needs, the architect Daniel Asher Alexander (1768–1846) was invited to prepare plans for expansion. In 1807 the East and West Wings were begun and in 1809–11 the colonnades which link these wings to the Queen's House were added. Thus, what are now the Main Buildings of

One of Alexander's Colonnades.

the Museum assumed much of the form they have today.

Across the road the Hospital was also accommodating and educating the children of seamen. In 1818 the Board of Admiralty through Royal Warrant became responsible for the Hospital, but three years later by a fresh Warrant the Commissioners of Greenwich Hospital assumed responsibility for the Royal Naval Asylum. Hospital School and Asylum were merged on the site south of Romney's road and the new Commissioners were confirmed by Act of Parliament in 1825.

To meet the needs of an increasing number of children, an additional West Wing was built by Philip Hardwick (1792–1870) in 1862. It is situated to the west of and runs parallel to Alexander's original wing. The gap between the two was filled by Neptune Hall, the work of Colonel Clark in 1873, as a gymnasium. Further work at the west end of the site followed in 1876 when Colonel Charles Pasley, Royal Engineers (1824–90), added another wing at right angles to Hardwick's. All of these additions were designed, from the exterior, to match Alexander's concepts of 1807. Neptune Hall is an exception, however, and its façade is in quite a different style.

The Hospital retained much of its old function until 1869 when rising costs led to its closure. In 1873 the Admiralty decided to rent the buildings and convert them into a Royal Naval College, for which purpose they are still used.

In 1925 the Royal Naval College, the Queen's House and the additional buildings were declared Historic Buildings and H. M. Office of Works assumed responsibility. In 1933 Greenwich Hospital School vacated the Queen's House site and moved to Holbrook in Suffolk.

The National Maritime Museum Act was passed in 1934 and this beautiful site was selected as a fitting place for the new museum.

The Queen's House, most appropriately, is the repository for a superb collection of seventeenth-century marine paintings. The West Wing, designed by Alexander, houses the Museum's Library, Globe Room and much of its administration. Hardwick's West Wing carries the story of the nation's encounter with the sea from the 'Glorious Revolution' to the defeat of Napoleon. Neptune Hall contains maritime industrial displays, and Pasley's Wing houses the Navigation Room, Restaurant and Department of Pictures. The East Wing carries on the story of maritime endeavour from the early nineteenth century to the present day. It also houses the Half Deck, or children's centre.

Meanwhile, over the centuries there had been much development on the Museum site now known as the Old Royal Observatory, where an unusually shaped building crowns the central knoll of Greenwich Park. It was designed by Sir Christopher Wren as the building to

Flamsteed House, seen through the Colonnades.

Greenwich Hospital, the Queen's House and the Observatory by Antonio Canal (called Canaletto) c 1750.

△ Alexander's East and West Wings from the north. The Colonnades connecting them to the Queen's House, the Old Royal Observatory and the rising ground towards Blackheath can be seen beyond.

▽ The façade of Colonel Clark's Gymnasium, now New Neptune Hall, of 1876. Alexander's West Wing is to the left and Hardwick's Wing of 1862 to the right.

△ The Royal Naval College today, with the Queen's House and Old Royal Observatory in the background.

▽ The Altazimuth Pavilion with the 'onion dome' and Flamstead House beyond.

Flamsteed House, the Meridian Building and the Great, or South East, Equatorial Building of the Old Royal Observatory seen from the west.

house the first Royal Observatory in 1675 and, with Charles II's approval, the site of Humphrey of Gloucester's tower was chosen.

The ground floor and basement of this unusual building were intended for domestic accommodation and the first floor, with its splendid octagonal room, was designed for use as the observatory. The first Astronomer Royal, the Reverend John Flamsteed (1646–1719), moved there from his temporary quarters in the White Tower, H. M. Tower of London, in 1676, and the building now bears his name.

The story of the Royal Observatory buildings is dealt with in detail in the chapter on *Astronomy and Time*, as they are closely related to the instruments they contain, for which parts of them were specifically built.

Although most of the work of the Museum is carried out in the two main groups of buildings at Greenwich, the National Maritime Museum also occupies property elsewhere. The magnificent Brass Foundry in the Royal Arsenal at Woolwich is pre-eminent among these. Designed and built by Sir John Vanbrugh in 1717–20, this is one of the oldest buildings in the country specifically constructed for heavy engineering activities.

Another property, owned by the National Trust, is at Cotehele Quay in Cornwall, where an eighteenth-century commercial office and warehouse now displays the history of the vessels and trades of the River Tamar.

The National Maritime Museum is extremely fortunate to have so many fine and distinguished buildings; and situated in one of London's most beautiful Royal Parks it lies close to the Thames, which for much of its history has been the country's most important waterway to the sea.

The Brass Foundry in the Royal Arsenal at Woolwich.

# Behind the Scenes

C. St. J. H. DANIEL
*Head of the Department of Museum Services*

The museum visitor exploring the galleries rarely stops to wonder at the mechanics behind what he sees, at how it is all done and when and by whom. A look behind the scenes will reveal how the displays in the galleries are created, and show the workings of some of the departments involved, such as the conservation, photography and education sections.

## The philosophy behind the display

Let us start with what we see in the galleries – the display. In the National Maritime Museum complex of buildings there are now some eighty galleries, including the small rooms in the Queen's House as well as the giant New Neptune Hall and the galleries in the Old Royal Observatory. There are also displays outside the Museum, in the various outstations such as Cotehele and

the Royal Research Ship *Discovery* on the Thames. All represent quite a challenge for Museum staff, especially as there is really no such thing as a permanent display. To remain alive a display should be updated or improved all the time, it should change with the times to meet the needs and arouse the interest of the public.

In the broadest sense of the term, a museum is an educational establishment, and the National Maritime Museum is no exception. It is therefore essential to remember this when deciding the purpose of the display and its design. The display must be informative, stimulating and entertaining. It may be that the new display will form an integral part of a chronological sequence, where other galleries have already set an historical pattern. At first glance this seems easy: just hang the pictures up and dump the exhibits down in the

The Weekly Inspection, which is a 'house-keeping' check on a particular part of the Museum – offices, workshops or galleries – to see that all is clean and shipshape. Here the Deputy Director, together with the heads of department and other staff, consider whether a display needs attention.

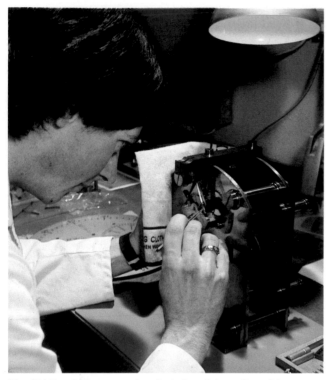

The Old Royal Observatory horological workshop. One of the specialist conservators works on the restoration of a clock, which may ultimately form part of a gallery display. Conservation Staff are concerned not only with the care and restoration of material, but with the environmental conditions of display and storage.

right order and you can't go far wrong, but in this way you ensure that one gallery looks exactly like another. In fact, when there is an historical, chronological order that has to be followed, the design scheme will be much more difficult than for a display which is a separate entity. The whole essence of the display must be first to attract and hold the attention of the visitor, and then to lure him on to further discoveries. To achieve this, there must be changes in approach for each gallery, so that each one feels different – changes in presentation of material, in lighting, in the texture of the carpet and in colour schemes, so that the 'taste' of each gallery is a new one to the palate.

## Planning

If this is the philosophy behind the production of an exhibition or a gallery display, then where do the ideas come from? They may be dictated by historical sequence to a certain extent but, whatever the case, the ideas usually emerge at a preliminary 'brainstorming' session held by the Director with the head of department responsible for a particular gallery and with members of the Department of Museum Services, which is the department primarily concerned with designing and setting up new displays. This 'brainstorming' session is likely to take place about two years before the new gallery display is due to open, and its purpose is to

establish the major theme of the display and the scale of the operation.

The next stage is to apply for funds to enable the project to be carried out. Let us assume that the gallery concerned is thoroughly old-fashioned, that new show-cases will be needed, the lighting is inadequate and that, in short, it needs complete renovation. This means a substantial sum of money has to be requested, with good reasons for making such an application – and this request has to be made a year *before* the financial year during which the actual work will be carried out.

The proposed gallery display now becomes part of the official Museum programme. The curatorial department concerned is asked for an outline brief of what they want included in the display and this is submitted with an overall scheme to the Director for approval. The wheels are now turning and the machinery which will change the whole face of the gallery is in operation.

At the hub of the operation is the Department of Museum Services, which is not to say that this department is more important than any other, but it is the responsibility of its head to co-ordinate the project as a whole. Inevitably, this involves many people and many meetings to discuss and plan the design, possible alterations to the gallery, lighting, showcases, exhibits and their conservation, display photography, publicity and literature. All these things have to be carefully considered and the final scheme put into operation and pushed forward in a regular programme until the exhibition is on display. The lighting, for example, is an important factor in conservation, which introduces us to the work of another primary department.

## The Department of Conservation

The Department of Conservation comprises twenty or so highly qualified conservators who serve the various curatorial departments of the Museum. The specialist disciplines they cover are in the conservation of water-colour and oil paintings, prints and drawings, ship models, astronomical and navigational instruments, fur-niture, clocks, books, manuscripts, sea charts and other archival material. The department is responsible for the welfare of all the objects in the Museum, with the exception of those archaeological items in the care of the Archaeological Research Unit. The head of Conser-vation advises curatorial staff on environmental con-ditions, recommending the optimum lighting, tempera-ture and relative humidity levels for their exhibits, an important aspect of Museum practice upon which the good condition of all the collections in its care depends.

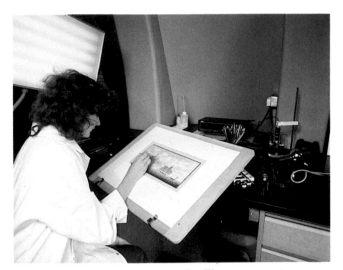

**Prints & Drawings conservation studio.** The conservator is examining areas of flaking pigment on this late eighteenth–nineteenth-century gouache of a cutter and a lugger by Charles Gore.

A Museum photographer at work in one of the galleries. As a major exhibition or display draws near, there is immense pressure on the Photographic Services Section to produce an infinite variety of prints to very high standards.

At present the conservation studios and workshops are widely scattered throughout the Museum, each workshop specializing in a particular area. The conservators are responsible for compiling condition and treatment reports for the objects they look after, and for advising on the origins and authenticity of new acquisitions by scientific examination. The various sections also carry out research into new methods and materials for use in conservation. Throughout the planning of a new display the Department of Conservation is consulted on the suitability of the types of showcase fabrics, on whether the objects themselves are in a fit state to be put on display, and on the lighting, to ensure that the radiation and heat emitted will not damage the object.

**Presenting the Information**

The displays have to be informative, and although some aspects are self-evident an explanation is almost always necessary of the display as a whole and its theme, details of a particular showcase subject and of each exhibit inside, and details of any other exhibits. This information is conveyed via labels written by the experts in the curatorial department concerned. It may seem an easy task; basically each label should be short and to the point, but therein lies the rub, for it is very difficult to write the kind of brief, informative label which invites people to stop and read. A great deal of work and

thought is involved before each label is passed to the head of department, Deputy Director and Director for approval before being printed, mounted and finally placed on display.

For almost every display artwork must be produced: one relatively simple drawing can often explain so much more than a long-winded label. The Design Studio graphics staff, working under the Design Services Officer (the Chief Designer) produce the various drawings and diagrams necessary to illustrate the different points the curatorial department is trying to convey to the visitor. If, as is sometimes the case, artwork has to be enlarged to suit a particular display or a photograph would carry the message more clearly, the Photographic Services Section is called into the operation.

This Section, under a Principal Photographer, is also a part of the Department of Museum Services. Normally, the staff of the Section are engaged in taking photographs or making prints for departmental record and research purposes, or as a result of orders placed by members of the public, but as the machinery for a new gallery display project moves into higher gear so members of the photographic staff may become involved. They work according to the exacting demands of the Design Studio to produce large prints, small prints, prints in black and white, sepia, colour and so on, all to a certain deadline.

Display Workshop staff completing the construction of a display panel, which will be set up in one of the galleries. Skilled craftsmen, they form the backbone of the Design Services Section, daily resolving the 'impossible' practical problems that arise in setting up a display.

Porter-Cleaners moving a piece of conservation equipment. These are the members of staff who fulfil the vital role of manoeuvring the heavy gallery showcases into position for an exhibition and cleaning the galleries.

Under the watchful eye of the Chief Designer, the display gradually takes shape on panels or in showcases. In the Museum's display workshop the fixtures and fittings, special mountings and other work are in hand. Meanwhile the gallery itself is closed, stripped of its old exhibits, rewired if necessary and equipped with the new showcases, redecorated and carpeted. Carpenters, electricians, decorators and the Museum's admirable team of porter-cleaners all beaver away to complete the construction of the new gallery. At last the display staff move in to set out exhibits, put up panels and labels and to add the finishing touches. Finally the new gallery is ready for the official opening, and the whole organization is already involved in the next display on the agenda.

## Public Relations, Publications and Conferences

All the expertise and effort expended in creating new displays and exhibitions would be wasted without the visitors, and it is the Museum's Public Relations Department that has the task of making the public aware of new happenings and developments. This small but highly professional unit handles all aspects of publicity: such matters as TV and radio programmes and interviews, films, liaison with all the communications media, the production of Museum leaflets and the three-times-a-year newsletter, *NMM News*. It is also closely concerned in the organization of such events as gallery and exhibition openings, and in the reception of important visitors to the Museum.

The Publications and Conferences Section of the Department of Museum Services is one of the smallest in the Museum, but also one of the most hardworking. There are usually four conferences or symposia held each year on maritime or scientific matters, most of them on an international level. On the publications side, there is also a wide-ranging programme of books, reports, monographs and technical papers constantly in the pipe-line.

The section is not always involved with a new gallery display, but now and again will play an important role if a catalogue or other publication is required, or it has been decided to hold a conference to coincide with the new exhibition.

## Education Services Section

We have already seen that the Museum is an educational estalishment, in that its role is to educate and inform at a variety of levels, from the provision of research facilities for scholars to actively assisting schools and informing the ordinary visitor through the gallery displays.

The Education Services Section, headed by the Education Services Officer, also comes within the

The tunnel which runs under the Museum, enabling staff and materials to move between buildings.

A school group in the Half-Deck studio. School children of all ages use the Museum's collections as teaching aids, and in this way gallery displays come under close scrutiny. Staff of the Education Services Section help to interpret and explain the displays, and guide children with their practical work.

Department of Museum Services, but the staff have no direct association with the production of a new gallery display. They are, however, interested in the end-product, since they may perhaps wish to produce worksheets for a school group to use when it visits the particular new gallery. They also need to know when the gallery will open so that they can keep schools informed, and they must be familiar with its purpose and contents so that they can talk to school groups about it.

In the East Wing of the Main Buildings of the Museum, in an area called the Half Deck, there are special facilities only available to school parties, including a work studio, a 'mess-deck' for eating lunch and a boat-building shop. On another floor there is also a large lecture-theatre where talks are given or films from the Museum's growing library of archival maritime films are shown. To help teachers decide which facilities will best

School children taking advantage of the Mess Deck, where groups of up to forty at a time can eat their sandwiches.

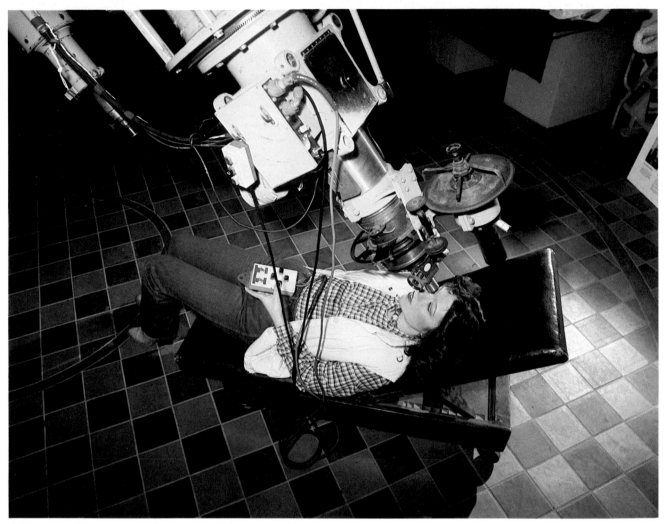

A Museum staff astronomer at the eye-piece of the 28-inch telescope. Astronomers of the Education Services Section assist or supervise observers using this great instrument, and arrange astronomy courses for students and teachers.

◁ The great 28-inch astronomical refracting telescope (1893) in the South East Equatorial Building. This is the seventh largest visual refractor in the world, and is still an operational telescope, used for double-star observations and for general observations by serious amateur astronomers, astronomical societies and educational groups.

suit their group there is a Schools Liaison Officer who will discuss the different needs and make the bookings for the chosen facilities. The Planetarium in the South Building of the Old Royal Observatory is in itself a constantly changing display and a unique teaching instrument illustrating the mysteries of navigation and astronomy. There, under a canopy of stars, the beauties of the night-sky can be viewed, and the motions of the Moon and planets demonstrated.

If the Planetarium does not seem to be entirely 'behind the scenes' it is but a step away, for when darkness descends on the Old Royal Observatory some members of the Museum Education staff may still be at work. They are the astronomers who may have been lecturing in the Planetarium during the day and who are now observing the real heavens. Perhaps they are enjoying a special privilege of working in the National Maritime Museum, the freedom to use the giant 28-inch refractor in the great onion dome. For with this splendid old telescope they can view on a fine evening the most beautiful and the most brilliant display of all.

The dramatic brilliance of the planetarium night sky. Schools,
university groups and members of the public can enjoy a variety of
talks and lectures in the comfort of the planetarium.

**Bronze Age Ferriby boat 3**, a fragment during excavation by E. V.  ▷
Wright from the Humber foreshore in 1963.

# The Archaeology of Water Transport

Dr SEÁN McGRAIL
*Chief Archaeologist*

The Archaeological Gallery is designed to tell the visitor about aspects of European water transport history from the Bronze Age to medieval times, a period of some 4000 years from *c* 2500 BC to *c* AD 1500. The Gallery is also a 'shop window' for the work of the Archaeological Research Centre, the department responsible for the Museum's collection of prehistoric and medieval boats and ethnographic boats and models. Whilst some displays describe early methods of boatbuilding and use, others illustrate the various sources of evidence available to archaeologists and explain the problems encountered and the techniques used to locate, excavate and record boat-finds and their associated artifacts, and to find out about the environment in which these boats were used. Research undertaken after excavation, such as dating, timber examination and the conservation of waterlogged wood is also described.

Early rafts and boats were made of reed, bark, hide, sinews and wood, all organic materials which readily deteriotate, and therefore it is only in special circumstances that ancient rafts and boats survive. Of the various types it is the plank boats and logboats (i.e. dugout canoes) that best survive the passage of time. Thus the Museum's archaeological collection is not fully representative of the range of early water transport, with no ancient reed rafts, log rafts, bark boats or skin boats. Nevertheless, the five prehistoric and medieval plank boats and the three logboats form a unique collection, representing types of water transport which must have had an important economic role in antiquity.

Ancient wooden boats survive because the timber becomes waterlogged. This characteristic becomes a hazard once the timber is excavated and removed from the environment with which it has (almost) reached equilibrium. If the timber is allowed to dry the weakened cell structure will collapse, causing the wood to shrink, split and fragment – in the worst case to the point of being unrecognizable as worked timber. Earlier this century various treatments were used in an attempt to prevent this deterioration after excavation, but generally without success, and boats excavated and conserved before about 1970 are usually unsuitable for display in public galleries. Nowadays improved methods are available and the two boats in the collection excavated in the 1970s, the prehistoric Brigg 'raft' and the medieval Graveney boat, are presently being conserved in the Museum's laboratories by impregnation with a wax, polyethylene glycol, a treatment which will take years to complete. However, during excavation and again during the post-excavation phase of research it is possible to copy a boat's features by casting in plaster, and from this produce fibre-glass positives for display. Thus, although the original timbers of the Graveney boat are undergoing conservation, a full-sized model is on display in the Archaeological Gallery.

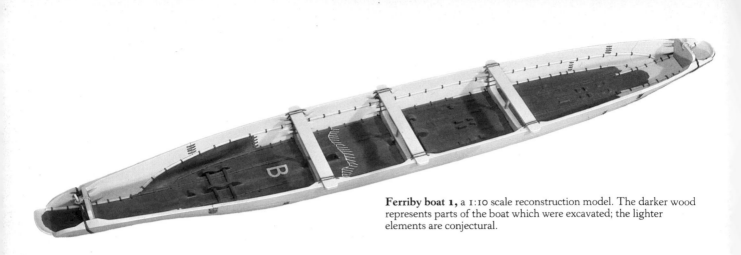

Ferriby boat 1, a 1:10 scale reconstruction model. The darker wood represents parts of the boat which were excavated; the lighter elements are conjectural.

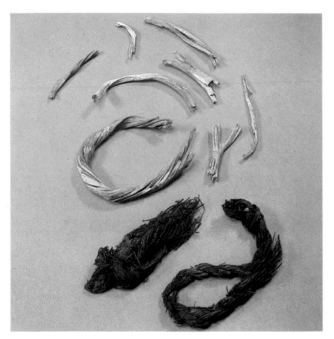

Fragments of yew stitching (*above*) and moss caulking (*below*) from the Ferriby sewn plank boats.

## The Ferriby boats

The three Ferriby boats are the oldest plank boats in Europe, dated by radiocarbon to the middle of the second millennium BC. They were found in the inter-tidal zone on the northern foreshore of the River Humber at North Ferriby near Hull in 1937, 1940 and 1963. After they had been uncovered from the clay in which they lay they were lifted in sections. Boats 1 and 2 are now in the National Maritime Museum's reserve collection, whilst boat 3 is in Hull Museum. The most substantial remains found were those of boat 1 and consisted of the greater part of the bottom of the boat and part of one side plank. The three oak bottom planks were about 15 m (50 ft) in length, stitched together with withy bindings of yew and made watertight by a caulking of moss covered with longitudinal oak laths. The planks were also connected laterally by oak timbers passing through holes in cleats which projected vertically from the planking.

From records and drawings made E. V. Wright during and after the excavations it is possible to deduce something about the missing topsides and internal structures of these boats. Three models, one-tenth the original size, which show different versions of what boat 1 might have looked like, are on display in the Gallery, alongside a full-sized diorama of the boat's excavation in 1946. The Bronze Age Ferriby boats were long, narrow, flat-bottomed craft, probably used as ferries in the Humber estuary and its tributaries and propelled by paddle and pole.

Archaeological Gallery, with a full-scale model of part of Ferriby boat 1 as she was during excavation from the mud of the Humber foreshore.

**Late Bronze Age Brigg 'raft'.** Archaeologists excavating from overlying planks so that the waterlogged boat timbers are not damaged.

## The Brigg 'raft'

The Brigg 'raft' was first uncovered in 1888 by workmen digging for clay near a brickworks at Brigg, north Lincolnshire. Some of the remains were removed at that time and the remainder reinterred. The site was relocated by Museum archaeologists in 1973 and the 'raft' re-excavated in 1974. From the post-excavation examination of the remains we can now recognize that this was not a raft but a flat-bottomed boat with features which are related technologically to the Ferriby boats: oak planking fastened by willow stitches, transverse timbers through cleats, moss caulking and longitudinal laths. Samples from the planking have been dated by radiocarbon to c 650 BC. This was a barge or punt-shaped craft used to ferry men, animals and goods across the Ancholme, which was then part of the tidal Humber estuary.

The timbers of the Brigg 'raft' are now being conserved in the Archaeological Research Centre. Meanwhile, a 1:10 scale model shows the boat as she was when excavated in 1974, and other displays discuss her original form and function.

Part of the oak bottom planking of the Brigg 'raft' after conservation with polyethylene glycol in the Archaeological Research Centre's laboratory.

**Late sixth-century Sutton Hoo boat.** The 1966 excavation of the boat impression by the British Museum. (Trustees of the British Museum)

Part of the National Maritime Museum's display on the Sutton Hoo boat. This is a fibre glass positive of the bow made from the plaster cast mould taken of the impression on site in 1967.

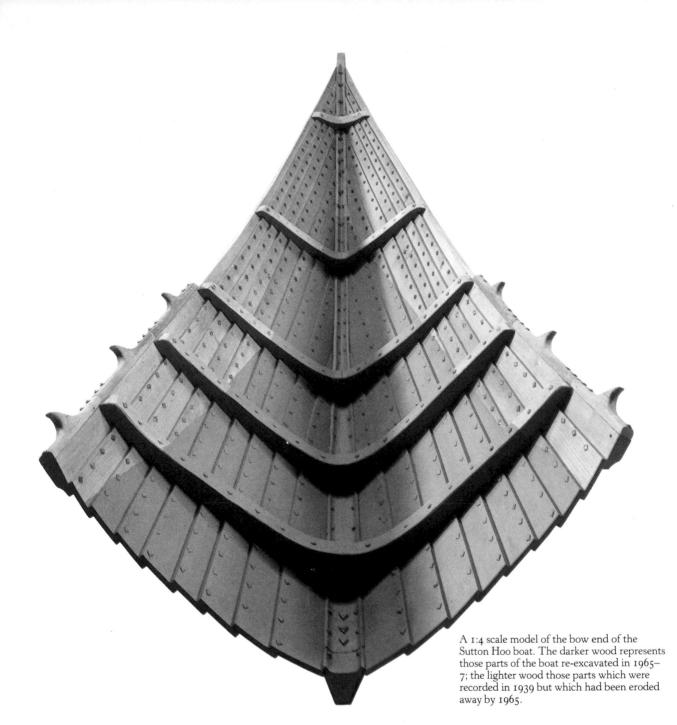

A 1:4 scale model of the bow end of the Sutton Hoo boat. The darker wood represents those parts of the boat re-excavated in 1965–7; the lighter wood those parts which were recorded in 1939 but which had been eroded away by 1965.

## Sutton Hoo

A large grave mound excavated in 1939 in the early medieval cemetery at Sutton Hoo near Woodbridge in Suffolk produced some of the most spectacular finds in British archaeology. They included the remains of a large open boat some 27 m (90 ft) long which had been used for the burial of (or as a monument to) one of the East Anglian kings of early seventh-century Anglo-Saxon England. During 1300 years of interment the timber had distintegrated leaving only an impression in the sandy soil of the mound, together with the hundreds of iron nails used in the boat's construction.

The site was re-excavated by the British Museum in 1965–7 and from this and from records of the earlier excavation the main structural features of the boat could be deduced. This was a clinker-built craft built in shell sequence, i.e. the internal supporting timbers were fitted *after* the shell of stems, keel and planking had been built; it was one of the forerunners of the style of shipbuilding that was perfected by the Vikings 200–300 years later.

A plaster mould of the boat impression was made on site and from this a fibre-glass positive produced. Part of this (the boat's forward-end) has been lent to the National Maritime Museum and is now on display in the Archaeological Gallery. Alongside this reconstruction is a 1:4 scale model of the same part with added features to show her as she probably was before burial.

The *faering* **replica** under oars during trials in Plymouth Sound.

## The *faering* replica

This boat is unique in the Museum's collection, being neither archaeological nor ethnographic, but experimental: a replica of one of the small boats found inside the late ninth-century Gokstad ship when she was excavated from her burial mound on the west side of Oslo fjord in 1880. The replica was built in 1972–3 by master boatbuilder Harold Kimber, helped by Museum archaeologists, and during 1973–5 she underwent rowing and sailing trials.

The *faering*, both in form and in constructional details, is typical of Viking Age building. Only 6.4 m (21 ft) long with three broad strakes on each side, she is a Viking longship in miniature. Trials under oars showed that the boat was particularly successful with a crew of two men each pulling two oars – as might be expected from her type name, *faering* or 'four-oared'. An impressive speed of 7.4 knots was recorded during these trials, indicating that the boat was probably wave-riding or semi-planing. On completion of the sailing trials, the *faering* replica was handed over to the York Archaeological Trust and she can now be seen on display at the Viking Age Coppergate excavation site in York.

Master boatbuilder Harold Kimber fastening a stem to the keel of the National Maritime Museum's replica of one of the small boats from the Viking Age grave at Gokstad, Norway.

## The Graveney boat

In late 1970 the remains of a late ninth-century AD boat were found during drainage work in the Graveney marshes between Faversham and Whitstable in Kent. A joint British Museum and National Maritime Museum team continued the excavation begun by the Kent Archaeological Society and lifted the remains.

Post-excavation examination of the recovered timbers has shown that this was a round-hulled, clinker-built boat, built in the shell sequence with a shallow keel-plank rather than a keel. The relatively full midships body with broad beam and the sturdy closely-spaced floor timbers indicate that she was designed to carry a heavy cargo such as stone; she may be thought of as the ninth-century equivalent of a Thames barge. Some of her boatbuilding features are in the northern European tradition (as seen in the Sutton Hoo find and the *faering*) while other characteristics may be of Frisian or even Romano-British origin.

The remains – about half of the original boat – are now undergoing conservation in the Museum laboratories, and a full-sized fibre-glass positive of the boat is displayed in the Gallery as she was during excavation. Small-scale models and diagrams indicate what the original boat was probably like and examples of the objects found with her are also displayed.

▽ Objects found with the Graveney boat: (*upper left*) rope fragment; (*centre*) hop seeds; (*upper right*) treenail fragments of willow; (*bottom*) fragments of a cooking pot, probably French in origin.

The Graveney boat display in the Archaeological Gallery. This is a full-size fibre glass model made from the plaster casts.

A 1:10 scale reconstruction model of part of the Graveney boat. The lighter wood represents conjectural elements.

Some of the late twelfth-century clinker planking found during excavations at Wood Quay, Dublin. (National Museum of Ireland)

**Early fourteenth-century Kentmere boat** during excavation in 1955. (Dr. David Wilson)

## The medieval ships from Wood Quay, Dublin

The Archaelogical Research Centre assisted the National Museum of Ireland in the recent excavation of a remarkable series of boat and ship timbers which had been used in the building of the medieval Dublin waterfront when the River Liffey was being embanked in the early thirteenth century. Some of these timbers, such as clinker planking, were still fastened together. A conserved repair patch is on display in the Gallery, together with further details of the excavation.

## The Kentmere boat

This medieval boat was found in the bed of what was formerly a lake at Kentmere, Westmorland in 1955. After being lifted, the remains were allowed to air dry slowly and were then conserved by coating with an araldite resin mixture. Certain parts deteriorated mark-edly and had to be replaced by modern timber but otherwise the boat is in a reasonable condition, albeit shrunken in breadth and depth and twisted lengthways.

This was a 4.3 m (14 ft) logboat extended by five iron-fastened, radially split oak strakes on each side. Four

birch ribs fastened by treenails supported this clinker planking and longitudinal oak timbers treenailed to the outside of the logboat base at the waterline acted as stabilizers. Shaped seats were fitted across the ends, and a loose ash plank placed convenient to rowlocks treenailed to the upper strakes was used as a thwart (seat) by the oarsman.

This hybrid logboat/plank boat has been radiocarbon dated to the late thirteenth/early fourteenth century. She is now dismantled and undergoing examination of her construction, load-carrying performance and stability.

**The Giggleswick Tarn logboat** in fragments.

The re-assembled Giggleswick Tarn logboat. The timbers in the foreground are now too distorted to be refastened to the boat.

**The Giggleswick Tarn logboat**

This logboat was found in 1863 on land which, before drainage, had been part of Giggleswick Tarn, near Settle in Yorkshire. After recovery the boat was allowed to dry out, but as she did so shrank, warped and split. In 1975 the boat was loaned by the City Museum Leeds to the National Maritime Museum: it was then in forty-five main pieces and many more fragments. The boat was subsequently reassembled at Greenwich and is now being monitored to ensure she remains stable.

The Giggleswick boat had been hewn out from a single ash log. Across the ends transverse timbers were fitted to prevent the log from splitting and to provide a seat for the paddler at the stern. Longitudinal timbers were treenailed along the sides of the boat, but near the top edge rather than at the waterline as in the Kentmere boat. These timbers were probably for longitudinal strength rather than as stabilizers.

The boat has been radiocarbon dated to the fourteenth century making her a near-contemporary of the nearby Kentmere boat. She is the youngest of the logboats found in England and Wales and so far dated, although there is a sixteenth-century description of logboats in use in Wales and they are known to have been used in Ireland and Scotland in the late seventeenth century.

**The logboats from Oakmere and Lough Erril**

The other two logboats in the collection are on loan from the University Museum of Archaeology and Ethnography, Cambridge and the Grosvenor Museum, Chester. The Lough Erril boat has recently been dated to the tenth or eleventh century by radiocarbon, but the Oakmere boat has yet to be dated by this technique, and the circumstances of discovery – at the bottom of a lake, with no associated remains – mean that she cannot be dated by other methods.

**The ethnographic collection**

The ethnographic collection, some of it in the 'Development of the Boat' display at the south end of the New Neptune Hall, consists of over 200 small-scale models of craft in recent use, and nineteen boats which were almost all working boats before they were acquired by the Museum. These boats and models come from all parts of the world, but while India and China are well represented, there are only a few examples from Africa, Indonesia and Oceania. Two early models of Mtepe sewn boats from East Africa are rare and important examples of this form of boatbuilding. Sewn plank boats have been used widely – in Lapland and in Chile and from the Indian Ocean to the Pacific – but it is only recently that they have been studied in detail.

Three of the Museum's collection of ethnographic craft, from top to bottom: a logboat (dugout canoe) from Haiti; a boat-shaped log raft from Lobito Bay in West Africa; a flat-bottomed boat formerly used to transport peat in Somerset.

The Museum also has a representative collection of skin boats and models from Britain, Ireland and North America, and examples of logboats and log rafts from South America and China, birchbarks from North America and logboat-based craft from India, Indonesia and Oceania. The remaining members of the collection are metal-fastened plank boats and models from several building traditions, in a variety of form and structure, showing the range of craft it was possible to build once boatbuilders began to use planks.

**Chinese boat model.** One of the Museum's collection is this Foochow pole junk of typical blunt-ended shape and with three battened lugsails.

# The Development of the Ship

Dr A. P. McGOWAN
*Head of the Department of Ships*

Tracing the development of the ship by means of the objects in the Museum is a fascinating exercise. For the most part, one is inevitably drawn first to the superb collection of ship models. Other collections can be used as well, however, notably those of the paintings and engravings, figureheads and boats. The important thing about the exhibits is that in almost every case they are contemporary with what they represent – as in the case of the models or paintings – or better still, they are authentic – as in the case of the figureheads or the state barges.

## The models

There is evidence that models were often used at the design stage by most of the maritime nations of Europe in the sixteenth century, but it was not until late in the seventeenth century that the Navy Board, under the Duke of York as Lord High Admiral, made models a standard requirement. The reason was simple enough: the Lord Admiral and the members of the Navy Board could not read plans and they mistrusted the seamanship of those who could, for such men were shipbuilders not seamen. When a new warship or class of warship was needed, the master shipwright at the dockyard concerned was required to produce a detailed model, usually at a scale of 1:48, so that the great men could see the actual shape for themselves. Occasionally the design was rejected completely, sometimes it was accepted as presented, but far more often it was accepted with alterations, the amended design usually being accepted in the form of a drawing. It is for this last reason that so many of the seventeenth- and eighteenth-century models can only be described as, say, 'a ship of 50 guns *c* 1715'; a model's dimensions can rarely be relied upon to conform precisely to the final draught or plan.

The nucleus of the Museum's collection of models came from the Old Royal Naval Museum, which contained the many Navy Board models retained by the Admiralty, and the private collection of the Museum's principal benefactor, Sir James Caird, who had already added to it the Mercury collection. These were also augmented by numerous models presented by private owners, a splendid practice which has been continued ever since.

## The sailing ship

The three-masted, skeleton-built ship, square-rigged on the fore and main masts and lateen-rigged on the

**Three-masted ship *c* 1480.** The earliest known illustration of a topsail in use.

mizzen, evolved during the mid-fifteenth century. This development made the handling of larger vessels possible and the trans-oceanic voyages of discovery practicable. The subsequent story of the sailing ship is largely one of the development of this rig to match the steadily increasing size of the hull, and the development of fore-and-aft sails to improve the square-rigged vessel and slowly to increase the size and efficiency of the schooner.

The first major distinctive type was the carrack, a cargo vessel-cum-warship with lofty fore and aftercastles, which made it an unweatherly sailer. During the sixteenth century the Spaniards and Portuguese introduced the galleon, whose squatter outline improved

*St. Michael* **90-guns 1669**
Dimensions: L gun deck 155 ft, B 40 ft 8 in, 1,080 tons; armament:
28 × 32 pdr, 28 × 18 pdr, 28 × 6 pdr, 8 × 6 pdr
Built as a 98-gun 2nd Rate, the *St. Michael* was reduced to 90 guns in
1672 but listed as a 1st Rate. The model probably represents her at
that stage. The bottle-shaped quarter galleries are typical of those on
warships built between *c* 1645 and *c* 1685. This is the earliest
identified English ship model.

**Ship of 50-guns c 1703**
Dimensions: L 129 ft 3 in, B 34 ft
The quarter deck of this transitional model shows the earliest evidence of the steering wheel. Before the introduction of the wheel, large ships were steered by the helmsman on the deck below using a whipstaff, a long pole pivoted at the deck level with the lower end attached to the tiller. The box with the forward opening to the deck gave the helmsman's head some protection and enabled him to see the sails and to communicate with the officer of the watch. On the deck below can be seen the rowle or pivot through which the whipstaff passed.

*St. Michael* **90-guns 1669.**
This detail showing the port side amidships gives a good idea of the workmanship in one of the oldest ship models in the world. The decorated entry port was normally fitted only on a 1st or 2nd Rate to be used as a flagship.

sailing qualities by reducing the windage. The advantage of this was seen by Elizabethan seamen, notably Sir John Hawkins, who developed the English galleons of the 1580s – the vessels whose manoeuvrability so surprised the officers of the Spanish Armada. The English galleon had much lower fore and aftercastles, better-cut sails and probably an improved underwater shape.

Early in the sixteenth century, topgallant sails were introduced and the spritsail was added to help balance the rig, and, by exerting leverage at the bow, make the ship more manoeuvrable. To this, the spritsail-topsail was added in the first years of the seventeenth century. It lasted little more than a hundred years and was more or less contemporaneous with the use of the whipstaff as a steering mechanism.

Ships had originally been steered by a tiller, but as they grew in size the tiller became unmanageable by direct control and from an early date it had required the use of tackles in any but the calmest weather. The whipstaff, a vertical stave attached to the tiller and pivoted at deck level above it, was a first attempt at solving the problem, but although it made steering easier it still did not allow for fine adjustment. The solution was finally found in 1703 with the introduction of the steering wheel.

**Queen Mary's Shallop 1689**
This most elegantly simple of all the State barges was built as a harbour launch to carry the monarch to a flagship or royal yacht. The fullness of the bow is in marked contrast to the design of the other State barges in the collection, all of which were built for use on the quieter waters of the Thames. The Queen's shallop is not only the oldest of the oared barges: it is also the last to have been used, bearing King George V and Queen Mary in the Victory Pageant of 1919.

**Lion figurehead 6th Rate *c*1715.** Only major warships, usually 1st, 2nd and 3rd Rates, had an individual figurehead. From the early seventeenth century until the end of the French Wars in 1815 the lion was the standard figurehead for all smaller warships. This splendid example probably adorned a sloop or similar vessel.

*Victory* **100-guns 1737**
Dimensions: L 174 ft 9 in, B 50 ft 6 in, 1,921 tons; armament: 28 × 42 pdr, 28 × 24 pdr, 28 × 12 pdr, 12 × 6 pdr, 4 × 6 pdr
This detail of the figurehead shows the scale and intricacy of the decoration used in a 1st Rate of the eighteenth century. This particularly fine model of an unusually large scale is said to have been commissioned for the court of enquiry investigating the loss of the ship in 1744. Flying the flag of Admiral Sir John Balchen, she was wrecked on the Casquets, near Alderney, with the loss of all hands.

**Prince Frederick's barge 1732.**
Designed by William Kent, this barge built for George II's eldest son displays all the magnificence of a 'floating coach', as Kent called it, for State occasions. Many of the motifs commonly used by the architect to adorn his buildings occur in its gilded splendour. The barge was last used by Prince Albert, the Prince Consort, in 1849.

*Royal Oak* 70-guns 1741
Dimensions: L gun deck 151 ft, B 43 ft, 1,224 tons; armament: 26 × 24 pdr, 26 × 12 pdr, 14 × 6 pdr, 4 × 6 pdr
Although the fourth 3rd Rate of the name, the *Royal Oak* of 1741 was listed as being rebuilt. The records suggest that few of her predecessor's timbers were of much value when that ship, of 1713, was taken to pieces. This probably accounts for the fairly unusual commissioning of a model for a rebuilt ship. Navy Board models were not commonly rigged, since all vessels were rigged according to the establishment laid down. It is most valuable in this case, however, as the rigging establishment was altered in 1745.

Almost coincidental with the first use of the wheel was the introduction of fore-and-aft triangular headsails on large ships, which enabled these vessels to sail closer to the wind.

Throughout the eighteenth century there was a gradual appreciation of the value of fore-and-aft sails in addition to square sails on large vessels. Staysails were introduced, and by the middle of the eighteenth century the lateen mizzen had been reduced to a quadrilateral sail. It soon became a boomless-gaff sail and by the early nineteenth century it had become the familiar driver sail with gaff and boom. Studding sails – which had the effect of extending the width of square sails – were brought into wide use in the eighteenth century, at the end of which another headsail was added: the flying jibsail, set to the flying jib-boom.

The figurehead was a distinctive feature on any warship whether it was the lion, the standard figurehead for much of the seventeenth and eighteenth centuries, or

**Bellona 74-guns 1760**
Dimensions: L gun deck 168 ft, B 47 ft, 1,615 tons; armament: 28 × 32 pdr, 28 × 18 pdr, 18 × 9 pdr
In Portsmouth Dockyard for a refit in 1778–82 during the period when the decision was made to copper the Navy, she was almost certainly used for experimental fitting. The model belonged to Sir Charles Middleton, the Comptroller at the time, and was used to demonstrate coppering to King George III and so gain his consent. It is the earliest coppered model.

**Cat-bark c 1760**
Dimensions: L 98 ft, B 28 ft, 360 tons
Cat-built ships developed in Britain on the north-east coast in the eighteenth century out of the Norwegian 'cats', used largely for carrying timber, and the capacious Dutch vessels that dominated the bulk carrying trades in the seventeenth century. The model shows the simple unadorned stem and absence of decoration that was typical of such ships. It is ship-rigged, but most of the type set only a fore and aft square sail on the mizzen mast after the middle years of the century, hence, probably, the descriptive term bark (or barque).

**HM bark *Endeavour***

Dimensions: L 97 ft 8 in, B 29 ft, 366 tons; armament: 6 × 4 pdr,
8 × 2 pdr (swivel)

The former Whitby built collier *Earl of Pembroke* was chosen by the
Navy Board for Captain Cook's expedition because of her stoutness
and capaciousness, common qualities in vessels in the heavy bulk
goods trades. Most important on an expedition to unknown seas, she
could be beached without strain, so that she might be loaded or
unloaded over an open beach at low water. The typical unadorned
'cat-built' ships were not normally square-rigged on the mizzen-mast.
*Endeavour* was rigged Navy-fashion after having been bought in.

the individual figurehead later accorded to ships of the
line.

Merchant ships were generally smaller than warships
and their figureheads less imposing. The chief difference
between the two types of ship lay in the shape of the
hull. Warships were built with fine underwater lines to
give them better sailing qualities, but speed and manoeuvrability were less important to a merchant ship than
being able to carry the maximum cargo possible on a
given keel length. Merchant ships therefore had bluff
bows and flatter floors (producing a flatter bottom)
which not only gave greater stowage space but also
enabled them to take the ground safely, deep water
berths being rarely available.

***Trial* 1791**

Dimensions: L 65 ft, B 21 ft 6 in, 123 tons

Drop-keels had been in use in various parts of the world, but this was
the first attempt to formalize the design of a vessel for their use.

Dimensions: L 144 ft, B 37 ft, 900 tons; armament: 26 × 18 pdr,
14 × 9 pdr
This model represents a typical 36-gun frigate of 1801–08.

From the first half of the eighteenth century onwards
there was a general increase in the size of merchant ships
of all rigs. The largest vessels were ship-rigged, but after
about 1760 an increasing number of three-masted
vessels adopted the rig developed at about that time for
the cat barks – the roomy bulk carriers from the north-
east coast in the coal and timber trades. Square-rigged on
the fore and main masts, fore-and-aft rigged on the
mizzen mast, this became known as the bark – later
barque – rig.

By far the greatest part of merchant tonnage came
from small vessels of less than 200 tons using a variety of
two-masted rigs. The square-rigged brigs and snows
were the most common, but the eighteenth century also
saw an increasing use of the schooner. Among smaller
vessels the ketch was prominent, square-rigged for most
of the eighteenth century but for reasons of economy
gradually changing to fore-and-aft rig by the first half of
the nineteenth century. In number, cutters, hoys and
smacks, each a mixture of square and fore-and-aft rig,
dominated the coastal trade until the mid-nineteenth
century, when the two former were displaced by the
more economical ketches and schooners.

HMS *Cornwallis* 74-guns 1813   ▷
Dimensions: L 177 ft, B 48 ft, 1,809 tons; armament: 28 × 32 pdr,
28 × 18 pdr, 12 × 32 pdr carronades
The *Cornwallis* was built of teak in the Bombay dockyard in 1813, the
model being made by the shipwright son of the Master Shipwright in
charge of her building. *Cornwallis* was converted to a 60-gun screw
ship in 1855 and after the Crimean War was used as a jetty at
Sheerness, where she remained until 1957. The model is shown
becalmed, heeling slighting to an ocean swell.

◁ *Ajax* 74-guns figurehead 1809.
The size of figureheads increased with the size of the ships. Compare
this figurehead of a 3rd Rate with the six-foot lion from a sloop a
hundred years earlier. The original figurehead of *Victory* in 1765 was
24 ft high and 8 ft wide. This more modest giant is nearly 13 ft high
and typifies the dockyard carver's work in the early nineteenth
century.

**_Tartarus_ paddle gun-vessel 1834**
Dimensions: L 145 ft, B 28 ft 4 in, 523 tons; armament: 2 × 9 pdr
Designed by the Surveyor of the Navy 1832–47, Sir William
Symonds, _Tartarus_ was officially rated as Steam Gun Vessel 1st class,
and was later used as a survey ship.

## From sail to steam

The development of the steamship largely depended
upon the ability of engineers to construct boilers capable
of withstanding increasingly higher steam pressures,
together with the development of a satisfactory con-
denser. By the 1820s the early work on steamships of
such pioneers as Symington (_Charlotte Dundas_ 1802) and
Robert Fulton (_Clermont_ 1807) had been developed to a
commercially profitable stage for short sea routes. Small
packet steamers were fairly common and the Royal Navy
used paddle tugs.

Although several steam-assisted vessels had crossed
the Atlantic before her, the first to make the voyage
under continuous steam power was _Sirius_ in 1838. These
early transatlantic steamers were all wooden paddlers,
but in the late 1830s the screw propeller was developed
by Francis Pettit Smith and John Ericsson, each working
independently. Their success was seized upon by I. K.
Brunel, who was then designing the _Great Britain_ (1843),
which as a result was not only the first major iron-hulled
vessel but was also the first such vessel to be propeller-
driven. However, although many companies turned to
iron and the screw propeller, the wooden paddle-steamer
continued to play a major role in the transatlantic
passenger mail services until the 1860s. There were two
main reasons, the first of which concerned the Admiralty.

**SS _Great Britain_ 1843**
Dimensions: L 322 ft, B 48 ft, 2,936 tons
One of the greatest products of the nineteenth-century engineering
genius I. K. Brunel, _Great Britain_ was the first major vessel to be built
of iron and the first such to be driven by the screw propeller.
Recovered after lying derelict for more than 30 years in the Falkland
Islands, the _Great Britain_ is now being restored at Bristol.

**SS *Agamemnon* 1865**
Dimensions: L 309 ft 4 in, B 38 ft 4 in, 2,212 tons
The introduction of the *Agamemnon* and her sister ships *Achilles* and
*Ajax* revolutionised long-distance trade. The new compound engine
enabled them to steam more than 8,000 miles without refuelling, and
the increased cargo-carrying capacity made the steamship profitable
on long voyages.

**Screw-frigate 51-guns *c* 1857**
Dimensions: L 235 ft, B 50 ft, 2,665 tons; armament: 30 × 8-in,
1 × 68 pdr, 20 × 32 pdr
The model represents the *Shannon*, *Liffey* or *Topaze*, three of a group
of four such ships built 1855–60. Coal consumption was high and the
engine was auxiliary to sail. When under sail power, the funnel was
lowered and the screw was disengaged and raised above the waterline
to reduce drag.

The Admiralty was responsible for the specifications
to which the mail ships were built, and in the 1840s a
series of unfortunate experiments led it to the conclusion
that iron was unsuitable for warship hulls. As a result the
first iron-hulled mail ship, the paddle-steamer *Persia*, did
not appear until 1856. The ban on the use of the screw
propeller for such vessels remained for a further decade.
The second reason was more technical. The engine in
use until the 1860s was the simple single expansion
engine in one or other of its forms, working at about
20 lb psi. Slow running, it was suited to driving paddle-
wheels but needed gearing to achieve the necessary
speed on the shaft to make the screw propeller efficient.

The principle of compound expansion had been well
understood in the early nineteenth century but compound expansion demanded higher steam pressures, and
there had been numerous fatal explosions because of
inadequacy of the boilers. Modest steps in the right
direction were made by Randolph Elder and Company
with *Brandon* (1854), and the Pacific Steam Navigation
Company with *Valparaiso* and *Inca* (1856), working at
80 lb psi. It was Alfred Holt, however, with the *Agamemnon* (1865) and her sister ships with compound engines
working at 60 lb psi that really made the steamship
economical. The new generation of steamships that
followed quickly dominated the most profitable trades,
particularly the tea trade.

**Coriolanus 1876**
Dimensions: L 217 ft 4 in, B 35 ft 2 in, 1,051 tons
The design of this famous vessel won a Gold Medal at the
Shipwrights' Exhibition of 1877. On her first voyage from London to
Calcutta via the Cape of Good Hope, she took only 69 days, the
fastest sailing ship passage recorded. *Coriolanus* was broken up in
1936.

It must not be supposed, though, that even the
development of the compound engine put an end to the
commercial profitability of sail. Although it placed a
limit on the life of commercial sail, in the short run it
actually boosted its value. With the larger sailing ships
built first of iron and later of steel, with iron or steel
masts and yards and using wire-standing rigging, the
sailing ships of the late nineteenth century were profitable in bulk trades that carried no market premium.
Coal, wheat, wool, nitrates and guano enabled sail to
compete with steam until the late 1890s when, with the
outbreak of the Spanish-American and Boer Wars,
freight rates rose at the same time as insurance rates on
sail tonnage were substantially increased on the London
market. The result was considerable investment in new
steam tonnage, and the sudden end to all construction of
new sailing vessels in Britain. Even then the phenom-
enon of the large wooden schooner kept sail profitable
for the next twenty-five years and almost exclusively on
the long runs of the American coastal and trans-Pacific
trades.

Improved steelmaking processes developed by
Siemens, Martin (in 1865) and Thomas and Gilchrist (in
1878) made possible the mass production of cheap steel
which was adopted for ship construction in the 1880s.
Equally important was its use in boiler construction, and
improvements in boiler design continued. The *Aberdeen*
(1881) was the first ship to be driven by the triple
expansion engine, which became the standard power
unit at sea for the next seventy-five years. The increased
efficiency of the triple expansion engine and the
widespread establishment of bunkering stations led to

**SS *Antonio Lopez* 1882**
Dimensions: L 384 ft, B 42 ft, 3,460 tons
Built by William Denny & Bros. of Dumbarton, this elegant
passenger liner bears the name of the founder of the Compania
Trasatlantica of Barcelona, her owners. The *Antonio Lopez* ran
between Spain and the West Indies and was lost after having been
run aground as the result of a fire in 1898.

**SS *Sizergh Castle* 1903**
Dimensions: L 361 ft, B 46 ft 2 in, 3,783 tons
Built as the *Scirocco* for the tramping firm, the Bedouin Steam
Navigation Co., this vessel typified the hundreds of tramp steamers
in service between the 1880s and the 1930s.

the development of the tramp steamer, which plied the ocean routes of the world collecting and delivering cargoes from one port to another. A great deal of trade was carried in cargo liners on scheduled services and many of these also carried passengers. The great passenger liners on the popular and profitable routes also developed in this period, in which the *Oceanic* (1870) marked an important step in being the first passenger ship to have the major part of her accommodation amidships, and the first in which it occupied the whole width of the ship.

Continuing improvements in boilers increased the steam pressures that could be used, leading to the introduction of the quadruple expansion engine and later, in 1894, the steam turbine. The expansive tendency in trade and shipping that accompanied all these developments led to the peak years in the British shipbuilding industry. Differing trades, attempts to minimize harbour and canal dues, restrictive safety legislation and the requirements of insurers led to the development of various designs of cargo ships: shelter deck, turret deck, raised quarterdeck and well-deck steamers are typical examples.

**Quadruple expansion engine.**
This splendid working model was built by the apprentices of Messrs. Green & Silley Weir Ltd. The quadruple expansion engine was a logical development from triple expansion as improved technology provided boilers capable of withstanding even greater pressure. Although these engines gave higher speeds they were not as economical and were only suitable in trades where speed was important. The most obvious of these was the passenger trade which, however, widely adopted the turbine after its success in first the cross-channel ferries and then in the transatlantic liners. The quadruple expansion engine was, as a consequence, used much less than the triple expansion engine.

**SS *Nonsuch* 1906**
Dimensions: L 350 ft, B 50 ft 2 in, 3,826 tons
The turret-decked vessels were introduced by Doxford's of
Sunderland in 1891 and were so called because of their superficial
similarity to the deck line of the early turret, such as the *Captain*
(1869). The unusual design gave an increased carrying capacity in
relation to the registered tonnage under the rules by which the latter
was calculated.

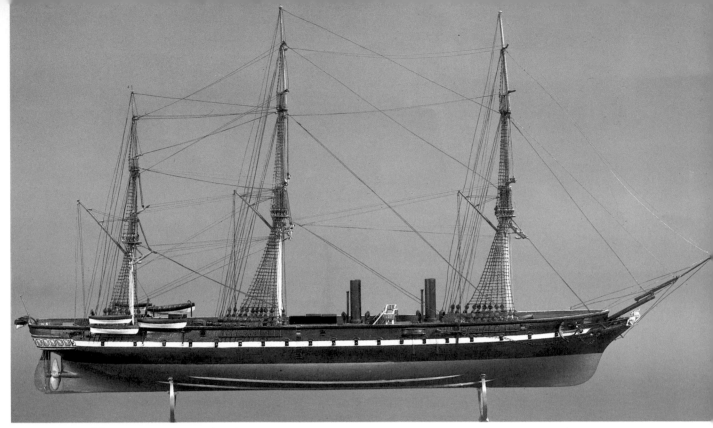

**HMS *Warrior* 1860**
Dimensions: L 420 ft, B 58 ft 4 in, 9,210 tons; armament: 11 × 100-pdr rifled breech loaders, 26 smooth bore 68-pdr muzzle loaders
The first iron-hulled armoured ships, the *Warrior* and *Black Prince*, were built as a response to the French *Gloire*, which carried iron armour on a wooden hull. When built the *Warrior* could have engaged any existing fleet in the world with impunity.

## Warships

The development of the warship proceeded on more conservative lines. The disadvantages of paddle warships led the Admiralty to abandon them, and by 1852 when the *Agamemnon*, the first major warship designed as a screw steamer, was launched a number of wooden ships of the line had been converted.

The value of armour against the new explosive shells was demonstrated during the Crimean War of 1854–6, and the success of the compound engine led to the construction of the *Devastation* (1870), the first major warship designed to rely solely on steam.

Developments in ordnance had prompted the contest between the gun and armour plating, with each having to compromise to avoid excessive weight. Increasingly heavier weapons led to a reduction in their number, but at the same time, with the abandonment of the broadside arrangement, the main armament had to be mounted on some sort of revolving chassis to obtain all-round fire. Similar constraints bedevilled the development of the cruiser, which was also required by definition to have a long-range steaming capability. The result was a number of only partially successful compromises, of which the descriptions first class, second class, armoured, and protected give some indication.

**HMS *Devastation* 1871**
Dimensions: L 285 ft, B 63 ft 3 in, 9,330 tons; armament: 4 × 12-in muzzle loader, later 4 × 10-in breech loader
The first major sea-going battleship not equipped with sail-power. The development of the big gun and the consequences of its enormous weight meant that fewer could be carried.

**HMS *Leviathan* 1901**
Dimensions: L 500 ft, B 71 ft, 14,100 tons;
armament: 2 × 9.2-in, 16 × 6-in, 14 × 3-in
This detail of the bridge and forecastle of one
of the large armoured cruisers shows how the
former had developed since the days of the
*Devastation* in 1871. It also shows how the
gun mounting which became universally
known as a turret bore little resemblance to
the original turret, and was properly termed a
hooded barbette (see *Devastation* 1871 and
*Ramillies* 1892).

After the initial technological breakthrough, much of the pioneering work in the design of boilers and engines was carried out by firms such as Yarrow and Thornycroft, specializing in fast small craft specifically built to use a new weapon, the locomotive torpedo, first produced by Robert Whitehead in 1866. This weapon meant that for the first time a major warship could be destroyed with a single blow. As a result, larger and faster versions of these craft, with an additional armament of light guns, were designed to act both as torpedo boats and as torpedo boat destroyers. Thus a new class of warship appeared: the destroyer.

However, the torpedo found its most effective carrier in the submarine or, more properly, submersible. Of the many names linked with the first practical submersibles, two of the most significant were the Swedish Nordenfeldt and the Irish-American Holland. A year or two behind its rivals in producing a submersible, Britain's first such vessel was the *Holland I* in 1901.

The chief effect of the torpedo on warship design was the appearance of the anti-torpedo bulges or blisters to protect the vital parts below the waterline. This outer skin was designed to take the main force of the explosion, protecting the inner more vital hull.

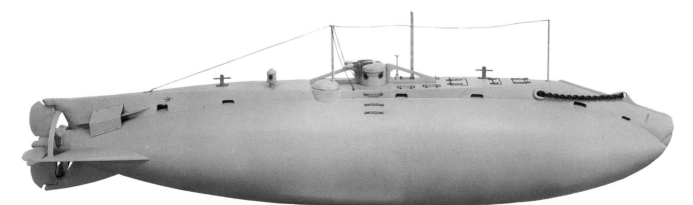

**Submarine boat No. 1 1901**
Dimensions: L 63 ft 4 in, B 11 ft 9 in, 120 tons
More properly called submersibles, as the first true submarine did not
appear until the nuclear age, the first such vessels in the Royal Navy
were of the Holland type, so called after their designer. The shape of
the Holland boats was more akin to that of the nuclear submarine
than anything produced in the intervening years.

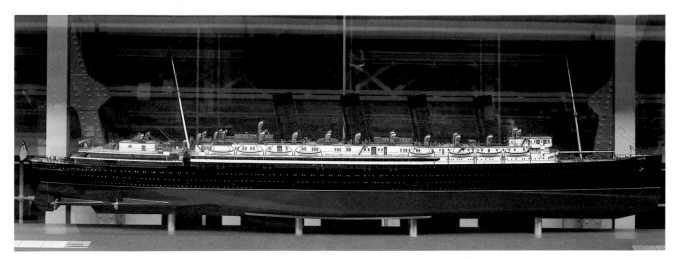

## RMS *Mauretania* 1906
Dimensions: L 790 ft, B 88 ft, 31,938 tons
The *Mauretania* and her sister ship the *Lusitania*, launched three
months earlier, were built to regain the Blue Riband for the fastest
Atlantic crossing and to re-establish Britain's supremacy in the
transatlantic passenger trade. Both ships were engined with turbines,
an act of faith by Cunard as few major ships, and no transatlantic
liner, had been fitted with turbines at the time when the great
Cunarders were laid down. They fulfilled all expectations. The
*Lusitania* regained the Blue Riband in 1907 and then saw it pass to
the *Mauretania* later the same year. The *Mauretania* held the
Atlantic record until 1929.

## The twentieth century

A major technical development of the years at the turn
of the century was the use of oil as fuel. The first
transatlantic crossing using oil was made by the tanker
*Baku Standard* in 1894, but the engines were not
economical and the fuel was very expensive. Oil-fired
ships faced the same need for bunkering services as had
the early coal burners, and steam engines using oil fuel
were not a commercial success until just before the First
World War. Meanwhile experiments were being made
using oil-powered internal combustion engines, the first
successful sea-going motor-ship being the Dutch tanker
*Vulcanus* (1910).

The steam turbine was first used commercially on two
Clyde ferries (1901–2) and two cross-Channel steamers,
the *Queen* and the *Brighton* in 1903, all built by Denny
Brothers of Dumbarton. Among the first to have
turbines installed were two of the most famous passenger ships ever, the sister ships *Lusitania* and *Mauretania*
(1906) of the Cunard Line, each more than 30,000 tons.

## M.V. *Silver Elm*
Dimensions: L 375 ft, B 52 ft 6 in, 4,351 tons
This model depicts a good example of the motor ship as it developed
in the years following the First World War.

**SS *Clan Ross* 1956**
Dimensions: L 502 ft 9 in, B 65 ft 9 in, 7,737 tons
A fast general cargo vessel, *Clan Ross* had deep tanks for the carriage of liquid cargoes such as palm oil, as well as derricks capable of an eighty ton lift for the movement of heavy machinery carried either on deck or in the hold.

Considerable faith had been required to put turbines into these great vessels; national pride was at stake as well as the reputation of the Cunard Line and British shipbuilding generally, for they were built with the express intention of regaining the Blue Riband of the Atlantic, held by Germany since 1897.

Between the wars the steam reciprocating engine was in the process of being gradually replaced in merchant ships by the diesel engine, which came into more general use in the post-First World War boom. However, the needs of the Second World War extended the life of the triple expansion engine as it could be more easily built and maintained than the diesel. The latter finally became the dominant machinery in the 1950s. The steam turbine was more expensive to run and its use was more confined to warships, and to merchant ships where the trade justified the cost.

Generally speaking, changes in the outward appearance of most ships were slight until the middle of the twentieth century. Motor ships were quite early to attain a distinctive silhouette with their squat funnels. The one markedly different outline appeared in the ships designed to carry oil in bulk, where for reasons of safety the machinery and accommodation were concentrated aft, and this design continued until the 1950s when it came into common use for coasters and nearly all bulk carriers. Because this design maximized the useable cargo space it was also adopted for the container ships which began to replace the conventional cargo vessels in the 1960s. At this period the square stern replaced the cruiser stern in most cargo ships, and new specialized vessels, for example, gas carriers and Roll-on-Roll-off (Ro-Ro) ferries, appeared each with its own distinctive silhouette.

The story of the warship in the twentieth century is very much the same. It had become apparent in the 1870s, with the adoption of an armament of a few very heavy guns on revolving mountings, that the best general layout on a warship was to place (from bow to stern) part of the heaviest armament forward with magazines below, the conning position or bridge with (later) the director tower above, then funnels with boilers and engine rooms below, more guns and magazines as appropriate amidships, and finally the remainder of the heavy armament aft with magazines below.

For thirty years following the construction of the *Devastation* (1870), the duel between gun and armour and the rivalry between navies led to battleships with an

**SS *Encounter Bay* 1969**
Dimensions: L 745 ft 9 in, B 100 ft 3 in, 26,756 tons
The *Encounter Bay* was built for Overseas Containers Limited for service between north-west Europe and Australia. One of the modern generation of cargo ships, she was originally designed to carry 1,300 containers each 20 ft × 8 ft × 8 ft. Subsequent alterations now give her a maximum capacity of 1,522 containers.

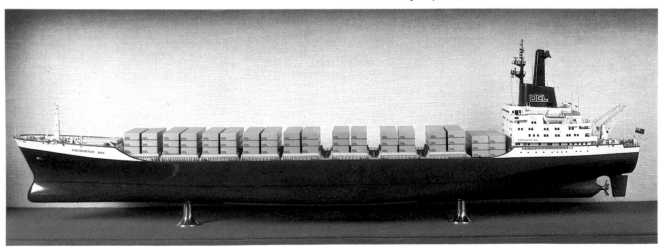

**HMS _Queen Mary_ 1912**
Dimensions: L 658 ft, B 89 ft, 26,500 tons; armament: 8 × 13.5-in, 16 × 4-in
The _Queen Mary_ was one of the ill-fated battlecruisers sunk in minutes at Jutland by the flash of a bursting shell penetrating the magazine below 'Q' turret, between the funnels.

armament ranging from the heaviest guns down through heavy-medium and medium guns, to light weapons used for defence against torpedo boats. Ammunition of different sizes complicated the problem of supply, whilst central fire control, with so many guns of disparate sizes, was impossible.

The problem was solved with the _Dreadnought_ (1906), with a rationalized armament of one-calibre heavy guns, one-calibre light-medium guns and at the same time turbine engines that made her faster than any other capital ship afloat. For a time she gave her name to all subsequent battleships and all 'pre-_Dreadnoughts_' were made obsolescent overnight. The layout had not changed when all battleships became obsolete in the years following the Second World War.

The same basic arrangement of guns and machinery held good for all surface warships. Appearances changed little between, say, 1912 and 1952. Cruisers developed into two types, heavy and light, depending upon their size and armament. Steam torpedo boats were replaced entirely by destroyers which served to attack the enemy battle fleet as well as defend their own from torpedo attack on the surface or by submarine. Because of their need to maintain higher speeds than their larger charges, destroyers and other escort vessels such as frigates were given a high forecastle to offer some protection in heavy weather. From the time they were required to remain at sea with the battle fleet in all weathers, destroyers have been built increasingly larger. This also applies to the 'destroyers' of the guided-missile age, and they have long since ceased to bear much resemblance to the torpedo boats from which they originated.

**HMS _Matabele_ 1937**
Dimensions: L 355 ft 6 in, B 36 ft 6 in, 1,870 tons; armament: 8 × 4.7-in; 1 (× 4) 2 pdr pom-pom; 2 (× 4) .5-in AA; 4 × 21-in torpedo tubes
The sixteen ships of the Tribal class were among the fastest and most powerful destroyers in use during the Second World War. The _Matabele_ was sunk in the Barents Sea in 1942 while escorting a convoy to Russia. The two pounder pom-pom was an automatic four-barrelled anti-aircraft gun, so-called because of its distinctive sound.

### HMS *Eagle* 1946
Dimensions (1964): L 720 ft, B 112 ft, 43,000 tons; armament (1964): 6 quad. Seacat missile launchers, 8 × 4.5-in guns
The model shows *Eagle* as reconstructed (1964) to include the angled flight deck, and a missile element in the armament.

Towards the end of the First World War the fastest torpedo boats were driven by internal combustion engines and operated from coastal bases only, and this has been the form of their development ever since. Experiments in aircraft carrier design after the first 'landing-on' in 1917 resulted in the single continuous flight deck. This type of carrier became standard in the 1920s, and armoured flight decks were introduced during the Second World War. Important post-War developments were the steam catapult, the mirror landing device and the angled deck, which prevented an aircraft over-shooting into the crowded aircraft parking area.

In the years since the end of the Second World War the warship has changed to meet new requirements. The battleship finally disappeared in subordination to the aircraft carrier, which soon lost its importance to the nuclear-powered submarine. Surface vessels were adapted to the missile age with guns retained only for policing duties. All welded construction replaced riveting (as it had in merchant ships) and wooden decks disappeared for ever. Diesel engines make warships instantly ready for sea, giving way to gas turbines when high speeds are required. The dangers of the nuclear age have led to enclosed bridges and no portholes. Tall, whip aerials have replaced the conventional aerials and warship silhouettes are dominated by the huge radar

### *Ark Royal* 1937
Dimensions: L 800 ft, B 94 ft, 32,700 tons; armament: 16 × 4.5 in, 4 × 3 pdr, 6 × mult. 2 pdr, 8 × mult. 5 m.g, 60 aircraft
This detail of the amidships section shows a Blackburn Skua dive bomber on the flight deck.

**HMS *Cleopatra* 1964**
Dimensions: L 372 ft, B 43 ft, 2,450 tons; armament: 4 Exocet launchers, 3 quad. seacat launchers, 2 40 mm
This model is shown as converted for Exocet missiles in 1975.

aerials. Almost every warship from escort vessel up-wards in size has at least one helicopter and a landing deck.

The last type of warship to be considered in the development of the ship in the twentieth century is the submarine. Of the first really practicable submersibles which appeared just before the turn of the century, the *Holland*, streamlined but tubby, somewhat porpoise-like in shape, was the type most commonly adopted. In the succeeding years, new submersibles were designed for the world's navies and invariably they became longer and slimmer with, in some instances, a surprising number of external projections which inhibited progress through the water. In the 1950s the first true submarines appeared in that, nuclear-powered, they could be entirely independent of the earth's atmosphere, unlike the earlier submersibles, whose diving time was strictly limited. It is interesting that the hull shape of this submarine is closer in appearance to the *Holland* than anything in the intervening years, even if perhaps it might be more aptly likened to a whale than to a porpoise.

**HMS *Scotsman* 1944**
Dimensions: L 217 ft, B 23 ft 9 in, 1,000 tons; armament: 1 × 3 in, 1 × 2 mm, 3 m.g., 6 × 21-in torpedo tubes
This class of submarines was reputedly very 'handy', being able to crash dive in 30 seconds. *Scotsman* was later modified for experimental purposes.

# The Story of Maritime Pictures

E. H. H. ARCHIBALD
*Curator of Oil Paintings*

In 1795 the Lieutenant Governor of Greenwich Hospital, Captain William Locker, suggested that a collection of paintings commemorating naval achievements and portraits of naval heroes should be established, and that the gallery where they would hang should be the refectory of the hospital, Thornhill's Painted Hall. The idea was not immediately taken up, partly because the country was engaged in the early stages of the Wars of the French Revolution, during which the most outstanding naval achievements were yet to take place. Indeed, it was the magnitude of these achievements which prompted a more enthusiastic response when the matter was raised once more in 1823 by Captain Locker's son, Edward Hawke Locker, who was at that time the Secretary of Greenwich Hospital.

King George IV was especially generous, giving the set of portraits by Sir Peter Lely painted for the Duke of York after the Battle of Lowestoft in 1665, and known as the 'Flagmen'; and also the set of portraits by Sir Godfrey Kneller and Michael Dahl of flag officers in the reign of Queen Anne, painted for her husband Prince George of Denmark, the Lord High Admiral. The splendid pair of battle pieces, *The Glorious First of June 1794* by Philip de Loutherbourg and J. M. W. Turner's *Battle of Trafalgar 1805*, were another gift from the King.

Locker successfully persuaded many naval families to part with battle pieces and portraits, and living naval officers, notably H.R.H. the Duke of Clarence, gave support with commissions. In a short time the first naval gallery in the world was formed, and eventually consisted of some 300 portraits and paintings of naval actions, mostly of excellent quality.

When the National Maritime Museum was established in 1934, this collection was transferred to it on permanent loan and formed the cornerstone of its collection of oil paintings. Of course, the Greenwich Hospital Collection was purely naval, while the interests of the new Museum embraced every aspect of maritime activity. It was therefore a most fortunate combination of circumstances that the Museum should open with the possession of copies of nearly every maritime print in existence. The collection had been created by the son of an Indian High Court Judge, Arthur George Holdsworth Macpherson. It comprised about 12,000 engravings of naval persons, ships, ports and naval occasions, and also a large collection of oil paintings, mainly of nineteenth-century merchant ship portraits. Its completeness made it unique, but in the 1920s financial considerations threatened its break-up.

Queen Mary took an interest, however, and in turn interested the King; both urged Macpherson not to lose

**The English fleet fighting the Spanish Armada of 1588,** oil on canvas, *c* 1588
This painting has little importance for marine painting, but a lot for heraldic and decorative art, and is probably by an English member of the Painter Stainers Company. The galleass in the foreground wears the standard of the Spanish commander-in-chief, the Duke of Medina Sidonia, though in fact the *San Martin* was a sailing ship of the 'great ship' type. On the right is a stern view of the *Ark Royal*, flagship of the English commander-in-chief, Lord Howard of Effingham, and on the left the *Revenge*, flagship of Sir Francis Drake, the English second-in-command.

◁ **The arrival of the Infanta Beatriz of Portugal at Villefranche in October 1522,** School of Joachim Patinir, oil on panel, *c* 1530
The Infanta came with a squadron of Portuguese carracks to marry the Duke of Savoy. The carrack in the foreground is the *Santa Caterina de Monte Sinai*, which was built in Cochin in 1511. These merchantmen, the biggest in the world at the time, were the first to have global potential. Bonnets are laced to her fore and main courses to give her greater sail area.

heart, and indeed help was soon at hand. By 1927 the Society for Nautical Research was far advanced in its negotiations with the Government for the formation of a national museum devoted to our maritime history, and it was realized how important an asset the acquisition of Macpherson's collection would be. Fortunately, too, the Society had a member who could do something about it. This was Sir James Caird, a millionaire Scottish businessman who had made his fortune in the Argentine meat trade and related shipping interests. He had already come to the rescue of the restoration of H.M.S. *Victory* when the scheme ran into financial difficulties by contributing £50,000. Now he stepped in and bought the whole collection.

With this and the Greenwich Hospital Collection alone the Museum-to-be would have been very strong in its art collection. However, in the nine years that followed the purchase of the Macpherson Collection until the opening of the National Maritime Museum, Sir James, who was working closely with the Secretary of the Society for Nautical Research and the first Director of the National Maritime Museum, Professor Geoffrey Callender, and with Jack Spink, the head of Spinks the art dealers, bought just about every worthwhile maritime

1591

**Sir Francis Drake** (1540–96), by Marcus Gheeraets the Younger, 1561–1635, oil on canvas, 1591
Drake was the second man to circumnavigate the world, in 1577–80. In 1587 he made a successful attack on the Spanish fleet at Cadiz, which was being prepared for an invasion of England. When the Spaniards came up the Channel the following year he was second-in-command of the English fleet that defeated them. In his remaining years he commanded expeditions against the Spanish both in Europe and America, and it was on one of these that he died, off Portobello in the West Indies. The painting depicts Drake wearing the Armada Jewel.

painting, portrait, drawing or print that came on the market, including about a thousand oil paintings alone.

It was as well that Sir James was buying and continued to buy paintings after the opening of the Museum and as late as the 1950s, since the annual Treasury grant for purchases for the Museum was then £350. In the early 1950s Sir James suffered a long illness and died in 1954, but purchases continued to be made from a fund that he set up, which enabled the Museum to acquire most of the paintings that it wanted.

**Queen Elizabeth I** (1533–1603), by John Bettes the Younger,
fl. 1575–1600, oil on panel, *c* 1570
Although Elizabeth was third in line for the succession at her father's
death in 1545, the early deaths of her brother and elder sister brought
her to the throne in 1558. The forty-five years of her reign that
followed were a period of great national resurgence and of maritime
adventures and discovery. She had the character and spirit to match
the times, and symbolized them for her people. In this portrait, the
importance she attached to her public image is expressed in the
sumptuous clothes and rich setting.

Things are now very different. Paintings which were
then purchased for two or three figures now command
four or five, and Sir James's splendid trust, once the envy
of sister museums, can no longer buy very much, while
our tiny grant of former years is now approaching
£200,000.

## The oil paintings

Good, early sixteenth-century pictures of shipping are so
extremely rare that the Museum is very lucky to have
been able to acquire the painting of Portuguese carracks
arriving at Villefranche with the Infanta Beatriz in 1521
to marry the Duke of Savoy, which is probably the finest
in any collection, though no attribution closer than
'School of Patinir' is possible. Likewise, portraits of
famous sailors of the period are likely to be hard to come
by. Even so the Museum has good portraits of Sir
Francis Drake, Sir John Hawkins, and a John Bettes the
Younger of Queen Elizabeth I. Also in this period is a
fine large picture of the Battle of Lepanto and two of the
Armada Campaign of 1588, one of which is apparently
by an English heraldic artist, possibly a cartoon for a
tapestry. Of James I's reign there is the great painting by
Pantoya de la Cruz of the Somerset House Conference in
1604 which ended the war with Spain. Of the King
himself there is a good John de Critz, and William
Dobson's sketch head of Inigo Jones, the architect of the
Queen's House, for the portrait at Chiswick House was
acquired.

**George Clifford, third Earl of Cumberland** (1558–1605), miniature
by Nicholas Hilliard, 1547–1619
When war broke out with Spain, Clifford threw himself into the
naval side, fitting out and commanding no less than six squadrons
against Spanish possessions from the Azores to the River Plate
between 1586 and 1598. He commanded the *Elizabeth Bonaventure*
during the Spanish Armada campaign of 1588, and personally
brought the news of the victory at Gravelines to the Queen, who was
encamped at Tilbury. At court he cut a splendid figure and was
expert in all knightly sports, and is here shown as the Queen's
champion with one of her gloves as a favour, wearing the star suit of
Greenwich armour.

**The return of Houtman in 1599,** by Andries van Eertvelt, 1577–
1652, oil on panel, *c* 1615
Houtman took the first trading expedition to the Far East, and this
painting records his triumphant return to Amsterdam. It is based on
the great painting by Hendrick Cornelisz Vroom, Eervelt's master, in
the Rijksmuseum, Amsterdam.

**The return of Prince Charles and the Duke of Buckingham from
Spain, 5 October 1623,** by Hendrik Cornelisz Vroom, 1566–1640,
oil on canvas, **c** 1624
At the instigation of the Duke, James I sanctioned an astonishing
escapade to further the match between the Prince of Wales and the
Spanish Infanta. Accompanied only by a Spanish speaking courtier,
Endymion Porter, they travelled incognito to Madrid. The
negotiations failed, mainly because of the Spanish insistence on
Charles becoming a Catholic. They returned in the *Prince Royal*, seen
here leading the fleet round the Isle of Wight and into Portsmouth.

**Peter Pett** (1610–?1670), by Sir Peter Lely, 1618–80, oil on canvas, 1637/8
A member of the famous family of ship designers and builders, Pett built the ship in the painting to the designs of his father, Phineas Pett. She is the *Sovereign of the Seas*, the largest and finest ship in the world at the time of her launch in 1637, and the prestige ship of King Charles I's navy. This unusual portrait is one of the few surviving pre-Civil War works by Lely, after the young Dutch artist settled in England in 1637.

This was the time when the Flemish school painters were in the ascendancy, and there are paintings by Hendrick Vroom and his pupil, Andries van Eertvelt, notably a very large Vroom of the *Return of Prince Charles from Spain in 1623*, whilst Eervelt's version of his master's great painting, *Return of Houtman to Amsterdam in 1599*, is in the Rijksmuseum in Amsterdam.

In Charles I's reign there was no great naval action except the abortive attempts in 1627 and 1628 to raise the siege of La Rochelle, of which the Museum has no paintings but two huge engravings by Jacques Callot. Instead Charles is better remembered for building up the Navy – the Shipmoney Fleet – which is well represented in an early portrait by Sir Peter Lely, *Peter Pett with the Sovereign of the Seas of 1637*, which he built and which is shown stern-on beside him.

The first of many naval wars, the First Dutch War, erupted in 1652 during Cromwell's reign. This led to the

**Scheveningen Beach,** by Simon de Vlieger, *c* 1600–53, oil on canvas, 1633
Simon de Vlieger was a key figure in the development of Dutch marine painting, and was the master of Willem van de Velde the Younger, and of Jan van de Cappelle. This painting depicts the catch brought ashore on Scheveningen Beach near The Hague.

**Robert Blake, General at Sea** (1599–1657), a miniature by an unidentified artist, oil, about 1645
Blake fought for the Parliamentary cause against King Charles I in the Civil War of 1642–9. In 1649 he was given a sea command with orders to find and destroy Prince Rupert's Royalist fleet. He found it at Cartagena in November 1650, and in the ensuing action only three of the Prince's ships escaped. He commanded the fleet at the opening battle of the First Dutch War in 1652, and by himself or in partnership at Dungeness in 1652, and Portland and the Gabbard in 1653. His last service was in the following year, when he achieved a brilliant success at Santa Cruz, off Teneriffe, by destroying the Spanish West Indian fleet. He died at sea within sight of Plymouth.

production of many paintings by Dutch artists (for there were no English ones) and the Museum has examples by Claesz Wou, Jan Beerstraten, Willem van Diest and Reinier Nooms, called Zeeman. Of portraits of the period there is a fine Richard Walker of General at Sea, Richard Deane, and an inferior but genuine and very rare portrait of Robert Blake. There are only three known portraits of him, and one of the other two is a fine miniature which the Museum also owns. In this period, too, are interesting paintings in the development of Simon de Vlieger's work, and the earliest known painting by Willem van de Velde the Younger, dated 1651, when he was seventeen.

The Restoration of Charles II took place in 1660 and the Second Dutch War began in 1665, when some of the better-known Dutch painters contributed their first battle pieces, such as Ludolf Bakhuizen's great picture of the captured *Royal Prince* arriving in Dutch waters after the Dutch attack on the Medway in 1667, and Abraham Storck's *Four Days Fight in June 1666*.

As a nation we are probably unique in collecting and exhibiting paintings of our defeats, and also of the enemies who perpetrated them; thus we have a number of portraits of Michiel de Ruyter, and also exhibit portraits of Cornelis Tromp and Egbert Kortenaer.

**Lieutenant Admiral General Michel Adriaenszoon de Ruyter** (1607–76), by Ferdinand Bol, 1613–81, oil on canvas, 1666

The most celebrated of Dutch seamen, de Ruyter emerges as the most able naval commander of the seventeenth century. In the Second Dutch War he commanded the fleet in the Four Days Battle in 1666, and was severely defeated at the St. James's Day Fight in the same year. In 1667 he took his revenge when he commanded the fleet that invaded the Medway, capturing Sheerness and burning and taking a number of units of the English fleet, including the *Royal Charles*. He commanded at all four fleet actions with the Anglo-French fleet in the Third Dutch War in 1672 and 1673. Although he did not achieve a tactical success, he avoided being defeated, and so prevented a seaborne invasion of Holland. He was killed in action with a French fleet in the Mediterranean. This portrait is one of several versions by Bol, one commissioned by the city of Amsterdam.

**The captured *Royal Charles* being taken to Holland, June 1667,** by Ludolf Bakhuizen, 1631–1708, oil on canvas, 1667

When de Ruyter invaded the Medway his most valuable prize was England's principal flagship, the three-decker *Royal Charles*. The Dutch never used her, but the royal coat of arms on her stern is preserved in the Rijksmuseum. Bakhuizen was one of the most successful Dutch marine painters, although born a German.

**A starboard quarter view of a Dutch built yacht about 1675,**
attributed to Gerard Valk, 1651/2–1726, wash drawing

There is, in addition, the set of thirteen portraits by Sir Peter Lely of the Flagmen who fought at the Battle of Lowestoft in 1665 – excluding that of the commander-in-chief, the Duke of York, which remains at Windsor, and that of Prince Rupert.

In the Third Dutch War period (1672–3) the work of the Willem van de Veldes (Elder and Younger) came to the fore. They sailed with the Anglo-French fleet in an English yacht in the campaign of 1673 in order to make sketches. The Museum has paintings by them of all the fleet actions, including the picture of the Battle of Texel which was painted for Admiral Cornelius Tromp, and which shows his flagship the *Gouden Leeuw* in action with Sir Edward Spragg's *Royal Prince*. It is the *chef d'œuvre* of all the Younger van de Velde's battle pieces and hangs in the hall of the Queen's House. Works by his father are also on display, for he was the greatest

**James, Duke of York and Albany, later King James II** (1633–1701), miniature by Samuel Cooper, 1609–72
At the Restoration of Charles II in 1660, James took up the duties of Lord High Admiral, a post he had held in theory since he was a child. He commanded the fleet that routed the Dutch at the Battle of Lowestoft in 1665, and at the less decisive Battle of Solebay in 1672. In 1673 he had to give up the post when the Test Act excluded Roman Catholics from public office, but resumed it when he became King in 1685, until the Glorious Revolution of 1688 finally banished him.

**Prince Rupert, Duke of Cumberland and Prince Palatine of the Rhine** (1619–82), by Sir Peter Lely, oil on canvas, 1618–80
Prince Rupert was the son of Elizabeth, Electress Palatine and briefly Queen of Bohemia and a sister of Charles I. During the Civil War he fought for his uncle, becoming famous as a cavalry leader, and in 1644 as commander-in-chief. After the war was lost he returned to the Continent and took command of what was left of the Royalist fleet, which was practically destroyed by Robert Blake in 1630. At the Restoration of Charles II from 1660 he held important commands at sea in the Second and Third Dutch Wars, culminating in the command of the Anglo-French fleet at the last three fleet actions against de Ruyter in 1673, the two Battles of Schooneveld and the Battle of Texel.

master of the art of *penschilderen*, or *grisaille* drawings as they are less accurately known. These are pen-and-ink drawings, usually made on a panel prepared with gesso but sometimes on canvas. They were done mostly in the 1650s, and by this method a very high degree of detail in the drawing of the ships was achieved. He later took up oil painting, probably taught by his son, and the paintings, such as the portrait of the yacht *Portsmouth*, have the same carefully-crafted, jewel-like quality of the *grisailles*.

The rest of the paintings in the Queen's House include four rooms devoted to the Palmer Collection of Dutch and Flemish paintings which the Museum purchased in 1962. The collection, which is all of seventeenth-century paintings, was assembled by Captain Eric Palmer to show the development and the inter-relationship of the Netherlands school, and is particular-

**The Battle of Texel, 11 August 1673,** by Willem van de Velde the Younger, 1633–1707, oil on canvas, 1687
This was the third and last fleet action of the season and the last action of the Dutch Wars. It was also the last attempt of the Anglo-French fleet to destroy the Dutch and so make way for a seaborne invasion of Holland. No major unit was lost on either side, but the battle was notable for the epic defence of the *Royal Prince* 100, the flagship of Sir Edward Spragge, Admiral of the blue squadron. That saga is already unfolding in this great painting; the *Royal Prince* 100 (*right*) is losing her mizzen topmast, while the man who commissioned this painting from van de Velde, Cornelis Tromp, is sailing into action in the *Gouden Leeuw* 80. Both admirals had eventually to shift their flags; but on the second shift Spragge's boat was hit and he was drowned.

**The Britannia,** drawing by Willem van de Velde the Elder, 1611–93
This English first-rate of 100 guns was built in 1682. In 1692 she was
Edward Russell's flagship when he commanded the Anglo-Dutch
fleet against the French at the Battle of Barfleur, and in the
subsequent destruction of the French fleet in the Bay of La Hogue. It
is one of hundreds of ship portrait drawings made by this artist and
his son.

ly strong in the works of Andries van Eertvelt and Simon
de Vlieger. Also, and on the whole devoted to the
seventeenth-century Netherlands school, though there
are a few English eighteenth-century paintings, is the
Ingram Collection room. Sir Bruce Ingram who, for over
sixty years until his death in 1963, was the owner-editor
of the *Illustrated London News* and the country's leading
private collector of Dutch marine drawings and paintings, lent the Museum a number of his paintings, which
fill a room in the Queen's House. The room, in fact, is
traditionally the one lent to the van de Veldes for their
studio. After Sir Bruce's death his three residual legatees
generously presented the paintings in the room to the
Museum.

The paintings illustrating the period from the reign of
William and Mary to the end of the Napoleonic Wars
are housed in the West Wing. There is a fine full-length
portrait by Sir Godfrey Kneller of Edward Russell, later
Earl of Orford, who commanded the Anglo-Dutch fleet

at the Battle of Barfleur in 1692, and at the subsequent
destruction of the French fleet in the Bay of La Hogue,
where James II saw his hopes of regaining the British
throne literally go up in smoke. This battle forms the
background to the portrait and is also the subject of
paintings by Adriaen van Diest and Peter Monamy.
There is also a full-sized, excellent copy by George
Chambers of Benjamin West's painting of George
Rooke and the boats of the fleet attacking the beached
French ships. Other paintings of this reign include an
equestrian portrait of William III with a background of
his landing at Torbay in 1688, by Jan Wyck, and an
exceptionally fine van de Velde the Younger of Princess

**King William III** (1650–1702), by Jan Wyck, c 1640–1700, oil on canvas, 1688
William was Stadtholder of Holland and King of England from 1688, first jointly with his wife, Queen Mary, and alone after her death in 1694. This portrait shows him on the famous white horse, which is in fact only a symbol of kingship; he rode a bay at the Battle of the Boyne. In the background his army is landing in Torbay to begin the Glorious Revolution of 1688. He arrived safely there because the east wind that brought him down the Channel from Brill also prevented Lord Dartmouth's fleet, loyal to King James, from getting out of the Thames Estuary.

**Sir Thomas Hopson, Vice-Admiral of the Red** (1642–1717), by Michael Dahl, c 1659–1743, oil on canvas, c 1707
In the War of the Spanish Succession, Hopson was a vice-admiral in the Anglo-Dutch fleet under Sir George Rooke, when it made its abortive attack on Cadiz in 1702. Fortunately, on the way home the news came that a fleet of Spanish treasure ships with a French escort had anchored in Vigo Bay, in north-west Spain. In the attack that followed, Sir Thomas led in the *Torbay* 80, which broke the boom defence.

**Thomas Mathews, Admiral of the White** (1676–1751), by Claude Arnulphy, 1697–1786, oil on canvas
As captain of the *Kent* 70 at the Battle of Cape Passero, off Sicily, in 1718, Mathews captured one Spanish ship of 66 guns. Again in the Mediterranean in 1742, this time as commander-in-chief, his fleet waited at anchor off Toulon for two years until the Franco-Spanish fleet came out to fight in February 1774. The result was a drawn action with only one of the enemy taken. Mathews was court-martialled, as was Admiral de Court, the French commander-in-chief, and he was dismissed the service. This portrait is one of four known paintings made by Claude Arnulphy of officers of the fleet as it lay off Toulon.

Mary arriving at Gravesend from Holland in 1689 in the yacht *Mary*, which is wearing the Protestant standard. The flag officers of this reign, and of that of Queen Anne, are splendidly represented by the set of three-quarter-length portraits commissioned (as mentioned earlier) by Queen Anne's consort, Prince George, the Lord High Admiral in the early years of the eighteenth century.

The first English-born marine painters, deriving from the Dutch painters in England, made their appearance in the early years of the eighteenth century, with H. Vale's picture of Admiral Leake's relief of Barcelona in 1706, and several works by Peter Monamy. Nothing is known

of H. Vale, who had a relative who signed himself R. Vale, but Peter Monamy (1681–1749) was London-born and based, and dominated the marine school and the painting of naval actions for the first half of the century.

Isaac Sailmaker (d 1721), who though not English-born apparently came to England as a boy and so is regarded as English school, is represented by the fine portrait of the *Britannia* first rate warship, and an interesting painting of the second Eddystone lighthouse painted in 1708 and on loan to the Museum. Associated with Monamy, but twenty years younger, was Samuel Scott (1701/2–72). He is the main contributor to the Museum's coverage of the War of Jenkins's Ear (the war

**A 1st Rate shortening sail,** by Samuel Scott, 1701/2–72, oil on canvas, 1736
The 1st Rate is probably meant for the *Britannia*, as she wears the flag of Admiral of the Fleet Sir John Norris, the commander-in-chief in the Channel in 1735.

between Britain and Spain which began in 1739), and painted incidents from Anson's voyage round the world in 1739–44 when he captured the Manila treasure ship, and his subsequent victory over the French at the First Battle of Finistere. There is also a pair of the Battle of Havana in 1748, and three very large canvases: one is of Admiral Vernon's capture of Portobello in 1740, and the others a pair of paintings, one showing the *Royal William* at sea and the other a Danish timber bark in the Thames. This pair are generally regarded as the finest marines by Scott in existence.

Paintings by a second generation of English marine painters make their appearance in this period and during

**The Capture of the *Glorioso* 74, 8 October 1747,** by Charles
Brooking, 1723–59, oil on canvas, *c* 1747
The *Glorioso* had just landed £3,000,000-worth of spicie and was on
her way to Cadiz, when she was sighted off Cape Finisterre by
Commodore Walker's 'Royal Family' privateers. Walker, believing
she still had her bullion on board, gave chase. The *King George* 32
engaged the 74-gun ship in close action for three hours, before
damage aloft caused her to fall astern. The *Prince Frederick* took up
the chase, and in the morning was joined by the *Dartmouth* 50, which
blew up in action, killing all but fourteen of her crew. Finally the
*Russell* 80 came up and took the *Glorioso*.

the Seven Years War (1756–63). For example, Francis
Swaine's (*c* 1730–82) large painting of a fourth rate
warship getting under way and excellent moonlit scene
of the *Monmouth* capturing the *Foudroyant* in 1758 are
exhibited. A Deptford shipwright and the father of a
family of painters, John Cleveley (*c* 1712–77), is well
represented by his launching scenes at Deptford, notably
his large canvas of the *Royal George* off Deptford (though
she never in fact came up to Deptford from Woolwich
where she was built and where he must have sketched
her). The best of all of this generation was the sadly
short-lived Charles Brooking (1723–59). He was certainly the finest English marine painter of the eighteenth
century, and arguably of the whole English school. He is

splendidly represented by a pair of action pieces showing
the capture of the Spanish two-decker *Glorioso* and the
capture of the French privateer, the *Marquise d'Antin*,
and ten more pictures of more general subjects.

One of the interesting aspects of the portrait collection is the number of paintings by artists probably not
found in other public collections in this country. This is
because the Navy of the eighteenth century, as a global
power, had firmly established stations in foreign places.
The portrait of Admiral Mathews, for example, is one of
three paintings the Museum holds by a French artist
called Claude Arnulphy, who managed to obtain commissions from officers of the English fleet lying off
Toulon between 1742 and 1744, waiting for the French
fleet to appear. A full-length portrait of Captain Edward
Hughes was painted in 1761 on a visit to Florence when
his ship was lying at Leghorn, by a lady called Violante
Beatrice Siries. The portrait is a beautiful fashion piece
but the ship in the background makes no sense at all.

The year 1748 had seen the introduction of uniform
for naval officers, though certain naval conventions in
their dress had begun to appear before that date, notably
the slashed cuff or mariner's cuff. The Museum is richly
endowed with eighteenth-century English portraiture,

**The capture of the *Foudroyant* 80, 28 February 1758,** by Francis
Swaine, d. 1782, oil on canvas, 1758
This fine new French two-decker was intercepted on her way to
Cartagena by the *Monmouth* 64, *Swiftsure* 70, and the *Hampton Court*
64, which gave chase. The *Monmouth*, sailing better than the others,
caught up with the Frenchman and an action began at 8.00 p.m. By
12.00 p.m. the Frenchman was almost silent, then the *Swiftsure* came
up, fired one broadside, and she struck.

including no less than eighteen portraits by Sir Joshua
Reynolds. Four of these are of his great friend Admiral
Augustus Keppel, the earliest dating from 1749, when
Reynolds accompanied him to the Mediterranean in the
*Centurion* when Keppel went out as commodore. The
second, showing Keppel striding up the beach after his
frigate *Maidstone* had been wrecked, was so unusual that
it caused a sensation when it was shown in London and
brought fame to the artist.

There are nine George Romneys, of which the full-
length portrait of Sir Francis Geary, with a background
of the fleet at Portsmouth by Dominic Serres, must be
one of the finest he painted. Among other notable
portraits are the full-length of Lord Sandwich, a First
Lord of the Admiralty, by Thomas Gainsborough, the
two three-quarter-lengths by John Copley of Admiral
Clark Gayton and Viscount Duncan, and the full-length
by Tilly Kettle of Rear-Admiral Richard Kempenfelt,
painted shortly before he was drowned when the *Royal
George* sank at Spithead.

The events of the Seven Years War were recorded by
Dominic Serres, Richard Paton, Francis Swaine and
Francis Holman, of whom the most important was
Dominic Serres (1723–93). He was born into a family of

minor nobility near Toulouse, was educated at the
English school at Douai, and ran away to sea. So when
he came to England and settled as a painter it is
understandable how easily he slipped into Society, which
was the main key to his success. His paintings cover
nearly all important, and many not so important, naval
historical events from the Seven Years War to the end of
the War of the American Revolution, and a mass of
other subjects. His nearest rival in painting actions was
Richard Paton, who could be excellent but whose style
was uneven, while Swaine and Holman were noted for
more peaceful subjects.

In the Year of Victories (1759) two big Scott paintings
show the futile attempts of the French to destroy

**John Montague, Fourth Earl of Sandwich** (1718–92), by Thomas Gainsborough, 1727–88, oil on canvas, 1783
The most enduring figure in the administration of the Royal Navy in the eighteenth century, Montague was first made a commissioner in 1744, and became First Lord in 1748. Dismissed in 1751, he was back from 1763–65. In 1771 he became First Lord for the third time, which proved to be by far his longest and most memorable period in office, covering the American War of Independence. He was also a founder member of the Hellfire Club, and invented the sandwich so that he could have something to eat without needing to leave the gaming table. This portrait was commissioned by Sir Hugh Palliser to hang in Greenwich Hospital, which is in the background.

**The Battle of The Saints, 12 April 1782,** by Nicholas Pocock, 1740–1821, oil on canvas
The chief aspiration of the French for 1782 was the capture of Jamaica. To achieve this Admiral de Grasse sailed from Martinique on 8 April. Initially he tried to avoid an action, but a couple of accidents in the fleet prevented this, and on 17 April the two fleets approached each other close hauled on opposite tacks. The English ships were copper-bottomed so held their wind better, and a shift in it enabled them to break the French line in several places. The Battle was a disaster for the French, who lost their flagship, the *Ville de Paris* 110, and had two more taken a few days later.

**Battle of the Glorious First of June 1794,** by Philip de
Loutherbourg, 1740–1812, oil on canvas, 1795
This was the first fleet action of the long French Revolutionary Wars.
Rear-Admiral Villaret Joyeuse put to sea in May from Brest to try to
intercept and escort a vital grain fleet from America for a famine
stricken France. He made contact with Lord Howe's fleet on 28 May,
and five days of manoeuvring and partial actions followed, until a full
fleet action took seven French ships, one of which sank; but the grain
fleet got through. In this great picture, which is over twelve feet wide,
de Loutherbourg combines two themes: the awesome grandeur of the
two great war machines, Lord Howe's *Queen Charlotte* 100 and
Villaret Joyeuse's *Montagne* 120 locked in battle; and the drama of the
sinking *Vengeur du Peuple* 74, with the compassion of the British tars
in rescuing their beaten enemies.

Saunder's fleet below Quebec with fireships, and Lord
Hawke heavily defeating the French fleet in Quiberon
Bay, a defeat made more certain by some of the escaping
Frenchmen being driven so far up the river Vilaine that
they could never be got down again. Richard Paton's big
picture shows the celebrated incident in the battle when
the French two-decker *Thesée* sank in action beside the

*Torbay*, commanded by Captain Augustus Keppel. This
officer was much to the fore in the naval side of this
War, and is shown capturing Gorée in 1758 in a painting
by Dominic Serres, and in a splendid series of eleven
pictures by the same artist on loan to the Museum, as
second-in-command to Admiral Sir George Pocock at
the taking of Havana in 1762, when his brother General
Lord Albemarle was the commander-in-chief.

In the next great conflict, the War of American
Independence, four new artists joined Paton and Serres
in recording events. The most important was Nicholas
Pocock (1740–1821), a sea captain from a merchant
family in Bristol. He came to be a professional marine
painter rather late in life but, encouraged by Sir Joshua
Reynolds, in time to give us splendid battle pieces of
Hood's action in Frigate Bay, St. Kitts, 1781, and the
*Battle of the Saints, 1782*. There was also Thomas Luny
(1758–1839) and Thomas Whitcombe (c1752–1824). Of
the latter's contribution the Museum has a pair of
paintings of the Battle of the Saints which belonged to

**Horatio Nelson, Viscount Nelson and Duke of Bronte, Vice-Admiral of the White** (1758–1805), by François Rigaud, 1742–1815, oil on canvas, 1777–86

As a midshipman in the carcass in the 1773 expedition to find a north-east passage over Russia, Nelson set off after a polar bear with a musket, so that we might never have heard of him if his Captain had not frightened the animal away. He was spared to become the world's most famous admiral. During the long wars of the French Revolution, he was present at four of the six great fleet actions, and commanded at three. In 1798 he took command, as rear-admiral, of the fleet that restored our presence in the Mediterranean and tried to prevent Napoleon and his army reaching Egypt. In this he failed, but in August 1798, at the Battle of the Nile, captured or destroyed all but two of the French fleet. In his last and most famous battle, Trafalgar, fought 21 October 1805, he was splendidly victorious, but was killed. This portrait was started when Nelson was a lieutenant in 1777, but not finished until 1786, so that he is wearing captain's full-dress uniform for 1774–87.

Lord Rodney himself, and a number of single ship actions. Luny's painting, *Battle of the Dogger Bank*, 1781, is on view, and there are versions of his *Moonlight Battle of St. Vincent*, 1780. The fourth new artist, Robert Dodd (1748–1815), not only engraved his own paintings but published engravings as well. On the whole, the engravings are better than the paintings, though there is a lively painting on view of the final stages of the action between the *Quebec* and *Surveillante* in 1779, just before the *Quebec* blew up.

Serres, Paton and Holman all died just before the beginning of the French Revolutionary Wars (referred to generally until after the First World War as 'The Great War'). It lasted over twenty years and saw the Royal Navy constantly and dramatically victorious over the French, the Dutch, the Spanish and the Danes, though with some setbacks from the Americans. Most of these events were captured by these last-mentioned four artists and also by a sailor artist called Thomas Buttersworth (1770–1867), and a Scot called William Anderson (1757–1837). In addition, there were Philip de Loutherbourg's three great battle pieces, of which the largest and most heroic, *Battle of the Glorious First of June* (1794), hangs in the Museum. King George III had bought it from de Loutherbourg's studio after his death in 1812, and in 1824 George IV had a companion piece painted by Turner of the *Battle of Trafalgar* (1805); both were to hang in the Ambassador's anteroom in St. James's Palace. However, the unpopularity of the Turner in certain quarters prompted the King to give both paintings to the new picture gallery in Greenwich Hospital in 1829.

**Rear-Admiral The Hon. Sir Fleetwood Pellew, Royal Navy** (1789–1850), by George Chinnery, 1774–1852, watercolour and pencil drawing
Pellew was the second son of Sir Edward Pellew, later Lord Exmouth, who took him to the East Indies in his flagship and made him a lieutenant in command of the *Rattlesnake* before his seventeenth birthday, and an acting captain before his eighteenth. This portrait shows him in the latter rank.

**The Battle of Trafalgar, 21 October 1805,** by J. M. W. Turner, 1773–1851, oil on canvas, painted as a pair to the de Loutherbourg *First of June 1794*, in 1824
This was the last great fleet action of the Napoleonic Wars, and the last to be fought under sail between European powers. Twenty-seven ships of the line, commanded by Vice-Admiral Lord Nelson, intercepted a Franco-Spanish fleet of thirty-three ships off Cape Trafalgar. This was strung out in line on the port tack, while the British ran down on them in two divisions. Because of the light wind, the leading British ships were badly mauled before they broke the enemy line in two places. In the action that followed, seventeen of the enemy were captured and one blew up.

Naturally the Hospital was anxious to acquire portraits of naval notables and succeeded at best with good originals, at worst with copies. Since then, as far as the latter are concerned, the Museum has in almost every case been able to purchase other good originals. Of some personalities such as Nelson and Lord St. Vincent, there are a number of portraits, and among the artists who provided them are Samuel Abbott (1760–1803), Sir William Beechey (1753–1839), John Hoppner (1738–1810), Gilbert Stuart (1755–1828) and, interestingly, some French emigré artists like Jean Mosnier (1743–1803) and Henri-Pierre Danloux (1753–1809). Officers were still being painted abroad too; there is a full-length portrait of Lord St Vincent painted in 1806 in Lisbon by Domenico Pellegrini (1759–1840).

The Wars finished fittingly with the downfall of Napoleon, which is dramatically displayed in three paintings. There is the famous deck scene on the *Bellerophon* by Sir William Orchardson (on loan from the Tate Gallery), with the Emperor watching the receding coast of France; the scene in Plymouth harbour thronged with boats full of people trying to get a glimpse of Boney, who used to show himself at the *Bellerophon*'s entry port, by John James Chalon; and finally, as if seen through a zoom lens, the full-sized, full-length of him in the entry port by the young Plymouth artist Charles Eastlake, who was in one of the boats in Chalon's picture.

In the century of comparative peace which followed the long French Wars, and which we know as the Pax Britannica, the emphasis in marine painting shifted to merchant shipping and peaceful scenes. On the naval side reviews tended to replace battles, though three very large battle scenes were painted: *Bombardment of Algiers* in 1816 by George Chambers, when Sir Edward Pellew secured the release of 3000 Christian slaves; the second, Philip Reinagle's *Battle of Navarino* in 1827, when Sir Edward Codrington's Anglo-Franco-Russian fleet destroyed the fleet of the Turks and Egyptians; and the third, the Bombardment of Sweaborg, a Russian fortress in the Baltic, during which the magazine went up. This was in 1855 during what is usually referred to as the Crimean War, and the painting is by John Wilson Carmichael (1800–68).

During this time of peace Pocock continued as the doyen of marine painters until his death in 1821. Thomas Whitcombe and Thomas Buttersworth continued painting until 1824 and 1842 respectively, while Thomas Luny and William Anderson lived on until 1837. Four figures emerged to dominate the second quarter of the nineteenth century. The first of these was William John Huggins (1781–1845), who was really already established and of whose work the Museum has

**Beaching a pink on Scheveningen Beach,** by Edward William
Cooke, 1811–80, oil on canvas, 1855
There is no harbour at Scheveningen, near The Hague, so the Dutch
hauled their heavy flat-bottomed fishing boats up the beach, or
beached them at high water.

**The Bombardment of Algiers, 27 August 1816,** by George
Chambers, 1803–40, oil on canvas, 1836
The Dey of Algiers held over a thousand Christian slaves, as well as
the British consul, and Admiral Lord Exmouth was despatched with
a squadron to free them. His Lordship's demands received no
response, so his ships positioned themselves against the Moorish
batteries, estimated at about 1,000 guns. The bombardment inflicted
tremendous damage, and rather than face a renewal the following
day, the Moors released the slaves, made peace with Holland,
promised to give up slavery, repaid ransome money to the amount of
382,000 dollars and released the British consul with an indemnity of
3,000 dollars and an apology.

a number of ship portraits and large paintings, such as
*East Indiamen in the China Seas* and *King George IV
aboard the Dublin steam packet Lightning in 1821.*

Then came Clarkson Stanfield (1793–1867), the
famous theatrical scene painter who also did marines of
such quality that he was regarded as the rival to Turner,
though the latter is too general an artist to be regarded as
a specialist marine painter. The Museum's Stanfield is a
fine late one of a lifeboat being launched to a brig in
distress near Dover. When Stanfield died, his place as
the doyen of British marine painters was generally
accepted as belonging to Edward William Cooke (1811–
80). He is best known for his Venetian scenes and Dutch
beach scenes. The Museum has a particularly splendid
painting called *Beaching a pink on Scheveningen Beach.*
Lastly there was George Chambers (1803–40), who was
the best of all of them but sadly died before he was forty,
like Brooking a century before. He came from poor
beginnings and the coal trade in Whitby to be the most
gifted marine painter of his day, and his *Bombardment of
Algiers* is one of the great marines of the century. The
Museum also has the oil-sketch and two drawings for it,
as well as another half-dozen oil paintings by him.

**The Grand Harbour, Malta, in 1888,** by G. Gianni, fl 1850–90, oil on canvas, 1888
The diversity of design in the capital ships of the mid-Victorian navy is well illustrated in this painting of units of the Mediterranean Fleet at anchor in Malta. The *Alexandra* (centre), launched 1875, was one of the last masted ironclads, painted white on orders of the commander-in-chief, Admiral His Royal Highness the Duke of Edinburgh, whose flagship she was.

When the nineteenth- and twentieth-century galleries were being prepared for opening in 1951, it was found that the picture collection was a trifle thin for the second half of the nineteenth century and the twentieth century up to the Second World War. Application was made, therefore, to borrow Chantry Bequest works from the Tate Gallery, which generously lent such masterpieces as John Brett's *Britannia's Realm*, a magical, extensive view from Beachy Head of sea and sky and small sailing vessels. Also on show is William Lionel Wyllie's busy Thames scene near Greenwich called *Grime, Glitter and Wealth on a Flowing Tide.* Wyllie (1851–1931) grew to be a masterly figure in the world of marine painting, and is reminiscent of the van de Veldes in his dedication to ships and shipping and in his prodigious output.

Apart from these loans, the Museum already had two important mid nineteenth-century works in Samuel Bough's painting of Dumbarton, executed in 1855, and James Webb's painting of San Sebastian. Since 1951 many late nineteenth-century paintings have been acquired to fill the gaps. Two more large Wyllie's of the 1880s, his best period, have been added: *Storm and Sunshine, a Battle with the Elements*, a dramatic scene of

a tug and barges by the powder hulk *Leonides* at Upnor, and *Well done Condor*, a brilliantly colourful portrayal of an incident at the Bombardment of Alexandria in 1882.

In 1959 the Museum bought from France a very large and colourful painting by Jules Noel (1815–81) of Queen Victoria's visit to Cherbourg in 1858.

Coming towards the end of the century, the Chevalier Eduardo de Martino (c 1834–1912) was marine painter to Queen Victoria and is represented by an excellent example in his *The Channel Fleet at sea in 1897.* In the same year the Queen celebrated her Diamond Jubilee with a review at Spithead, of which there is a large oil painting by Charles Dixon (1872–1934).

In the Edwardian era and leading up to the First World War, Wyllie continued to dominate the marine painting scene and the Museum has a large painting of the visit of the French Fleet to Spithead in 1905. Another painter, Alma Burlton Cull, was concentrating on Royal Naval subjects, and there are two large paintings by him of the *King Edward VII class battleships at sea*, showing why they were known as 'The Wobbly Eight', and another of the Fleet gathered at Spithead before King George V's Coronation Review in 1911.

**Thames barges and shipping off Gravesend,** by William Lionel
Wyllie, 1851–1931, wash drawing

**King Edward VII class battleships at sea in 1912,** by Alma Burlton
Cull, 1880–1931, oil on canvas, 1912
This class had a peculiarity evident in the painting; they steered
slightly crabwise, so that they were known as the Wobbly Eight. This
painting was commissioned by the Prince of Wales who was serving
as a midshipman in the leading ship, the *Hindustan*.

**The *Wiscombe Park* running her easting down in the South Atlantic,** by John Everett, 1876–1949, pastel, *c* 1920

Because another national museum, the Imperial War Museum, was formed specifically to cover the First World War in all its aspects, this Museum made little effort until recent years to acquire paintings of its events. However, the presentation of the War has been given a significant boost by the acquisition of two very large paintings. One is on loan from the National Portrait Gallery and is the great portrait group set in the Board Room of the Admiralty of flag officers who fought in the War, by Sir Arthur Cope (1851–1940). The second is of the most important naval event of the War, the surrender of the German High Seas Fleet, which is shown being led by the cruiser *Cardiff* between two lines of the Grand Fleet, including the American Battle Squadron. This picture formerly hung in the Cardiff Coal Exchange and is by Charles Dixon.

The marine painters who began their careers at the turn of the century, such as Norman Wilkinson and Charles Pears, are chiefly represented by their work in the Second World War (though there are a few early works). Although the Imperial War Museum's mandate was enlarged to embrace the Second as well as the First World War, this Museum received the bulk of the paintings of naval interest, which included actions and portraits painted for the War Artists Commission, for which Pears painted and Wilkinson did not. Instead, Wilkinson painted fifty canvases which he called *The War at Sea* and presented to the nation. He wanted them to be kept together at Greenwich, but there was opposition to this from those who thought they should be shared among the galleries. In the end Wilkinson sought the help of Clement Atlee, then Prime Minister, who gave a ruling that they should all be kept together at Greenwich. Other artists represented among the War Artists were Charles Cundall, Muirhead and Stephen Bone, Bernard Freedman and Charles Pitchforth.

A Society of Marine Artists was formed just after the Second World War, and its members' diploma works are kept on permanent loan in the Museum, ensuring a wide coverage of contemporary paintings. The Museum also buys a painting every year from this exhibition, and is presented with a financial contribution from the Society.

### Prints and drawings

Since paper and watercolours deteriorate in light, these collections are not intended for permanent displays but rather for special, temporary exhibitions, for study and for information on the subjects they cover. They are normally kept in solander boxes: the prints are arranged by subject; the portraits by date of death of the sitter; and the ship portraits by date of launch, sub-divided into merchant sailing ships, merchant steam ships, yachts and fighting ships. The prints of actions and historical subjects are arranged chronologically and the seaports to their places in the old *Times Gazetteer*. The watercolours and drawings are arranged chronologically under the date of death of the artists, and of these the most important of the three largest collections are some 1400 drawings by the Elder and Younger Willem van de Veldes. Approximately half of these were purchased over the years by Sir James Caird and the other half presented by Sir Bruce Ingram to mark his fiftieth year as owner-editor of the *Illustrated London News*. As the majority of them are named ship portraits of Dutch, English, French and Swedish ships, they constitute a unique coverage of the subject.

The second very large collection is that of drawings from William Lionel Wyllie's studio, purchased from his family by Sir James Caird in 1931 and numbering some 7000 watercolours. Wyllie lived most of his working life first in Rochester and later in Tower House overlooking the entrance to Portsmouth Harbour, so the bulk of his vast output is devoted to shipping in the Thames and the work of the Royal Navy, with which he became closely associated.

The third big collection is the maritime work of an artist called John Everett (1876–1949), who was little-known since he did not exhibit or try to sell his work. He was a pupil at the Slade School in the 1890s with Augustus John and William Orpen, who lodged in his mother's house. In 1899 he travelled round the world in a sailing ship and also made subsequent voyages. Consequently much of his work is of deck scenes. He also painted yachting and dazzle-painted (camouflaged) ships in the First World War. In all, the collection, which was bequeathed to the Museum, consists of about 2000 drawings, many in pastel, aquatints with their plates, and 1600 oil-paintings.

Another large collection is of the watercolours of Alma Cull (d 1928), bequeathed by his widow in 1954. These are rather like Wyllie's work and nearly all of Royal Naval subjects. The Museum also purchased in the 1950s the considerable remains of the studio of John Fraser (1858–1927). This artist's work is so similar to that of de Martino's that he used to execute some of that artist's commissions, who would then work on them a little, sign them and pass them off as his own.

The rest of the collection of watercolours and drawings is so large and varied, including as it does examples of most acknowledged marine painters, that it

The stern of the *Aquitania*, Bedford-Lemere Collection, 1914
The *Aquitania* is here shown in dry dock, just before she went into service on the North Atlantic run in 1914, the start of a working life that was to span nearly forty years.

◁ The *Great Britain* fitting out at Bristol in 1843
This early photograph was printed from a paper negative developed by Willam Henry Fox-Talbot, 1800–77, who called the pictures calotypes. The Museum has a collection of his negatives.

is difficult to single artists out. However, there is a large collection of watercolours and drawings by Nicholas Pocock, the majority of which were pencil drawings for his paintings, and a collection of large watercolours by another seaman painter, Thomas Buttersworth, especially of the blockade of Cadiz in 1797 at which he was probably present. Among the portrait drawings are two very fine full-sized pastels by John Russell (1745–1806) of Captain Pierrepoint and his wife. Portraits by George Chinnery (1774–1852) and Henry Eldridge (1769–1821) are also included.

The foundation of the collection of prints was the acquisition of the Macpherson Collection in 1928, and to this was added the highly comprehensive collection of engravings of naval actions which had been made by Sir Charles Cust, the W. T. Spencer Collection and the Caldwell Collection of mezzotint portraits. In all, the collection of prints and drawings numbers about 30,000 items.

## Photographs
Since before the Second World War, photographs of paintings and portraits were collected and housed in solander boxes under the date of death of the artist, or the date of death of the subjects of the portraits, which include actual photographs of people. At present there are about 12,000 mounted photographs of marine paintings and drawings and 6000 portraits.

◁ The library of the North Atlantic liner *Lucania*
Built for the Cunard Company in 1893, *Lucania* was, with her sister the *Campania*, the largest and fastest passenger liner in the world for six years. This print is from a large collection of glass negatives made by the firm of Glasgow photographers, Bedford-Lemere, which for many years was the leading firm specialising in ship interiors.

## The Archive of Historic Photographs
In 1947, at the instigation of the Society for Nautical Research and on the initiative of the present Director of the Museum, Basil Greenhill, the Museum began to collect prints and negatives of every kind of nautical activity from the beginnings of photography in the nineteenth century to the present day. This became by far the fastest growing section of the department and now contains some half a million items. The work of mounting and filing the collection was initially undertaken by the printroom staff, but as the collection grew a special Historic Photograph Section was formed within the department to look after it.

Generous gifts over the years have made this the most comprehensive source of maritime illustration in the world. Among its collections are Fox Talbot's paper negatives of the 1840s, 20,000 negatives of merchant sail and steam that comprised the Nautical Photo Agency, the Richard Perkins collection of about 11,000 negatives of warships, the Gould Collection of negatives of nineteenth-century shipping at Gravesend, and the Bedford Lemere collection of ocean liner interiors.

# Navigation and Hydrography

The science and practice of navigation is an essential element in the story of man's encounter with the sea. However well built his ships, without the ability to navigate he would have lacked the confidence to explore, would have been unable to fix and relocate newly discovered lands and would have found it too hazardous to use the oceans as a means of establishing commerce with foreign countries. Indeed the science of navigation has had a direct effect on world history; communication between peoples otherwise separated by the oceans resulted in the interaction of cultures, the spread of knowledge and ideas, the great migrations and the subjugation and destruction of races.

The collections in the National Maritime Museum of artefacts, documents and records covering the history of navigation are unrivalled. In this chapter, the subject has been divided into two sections so that hydrography and the development of the chart is described separately from the instruments used by navigators and surveyors. It must be remembered that the art of navigation involves the combined use of charts and instruments and that the successful use of both relies heavily on data provided by the shore-based astronomer.

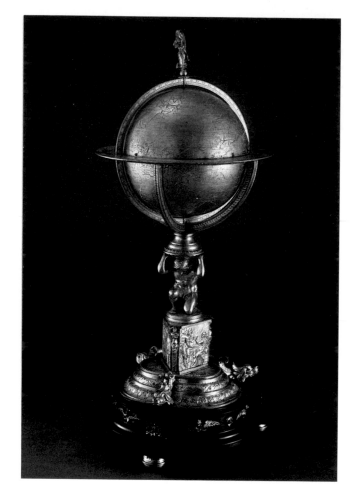

**Gilt terrestial globe** made in 1597 by Cristoph Schissler of Augsburg, one of the most famous of European instrument makers.

## The Hydrographic Collection

### CHRISTOPHER TERRELL
*Curator of Hydrography*

The science of hydrography – the methodical recording of navigational information for the mariner in chart and pilot book – is as old as that of navigation itself. The hydrographic collections at Greenwich contain an historic record of this endeavour from the earliest times to the present day.

The emergence of the magnetic compass in the hands of the Mediterranean navigator in the twelfth century was the key to the accurate recording of information, and it is from this period that the earliest sea charts survive.

Hand-drawn on vellum, they initially covered the Mediterranean basin and the sea routes to northern Europe. Later, following the great Portuguese and Spanish voyages of discovery of the fifteenth and sixteenth centuries, they gradually extended their cover to the Atlantic and Indian Oceans. Several fine examples of these beautifully drawn and illuminated charts are preserved at Greenwich.

In the sixteenth century the invention of printing transformed the chart trade, enabling production in greater numbers, more cheaply and without copyist's errors. The technique of printing from engraved copper plates, first developed in Italy, proved ideal for recording the mass of small detail necessary on a nautical chart. Coinciding as it did with the rise of the Dutch seaborne empire, the process was quickly adopted by them, and the publishing houses of Amsterdam were to dominate chart and map production for a century. The charts were

**Celestial Globe** by Gemma Frisius, 1537. The museum has a collection of over 230 globes, one of the largest and most comprehensive in the world. This example by the Dutch astronomer Gemma 'the Frisian' is the oldest in the collection.

**The Island of Crete** by Bartolommeo Dalli Sonetti, *c* 1485. This manuscript chart, drawn by a Venetian shipmaster, is one of the earliest examples in the Museum.

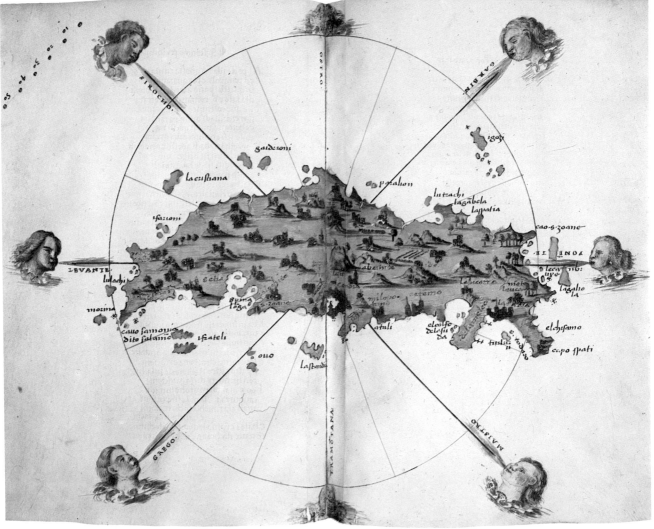

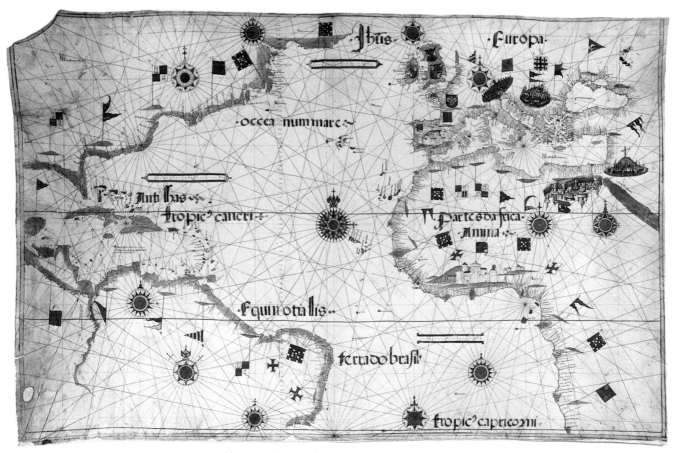

**Portuguese chart of the North Atlantic** by Pedro Reinel, *c* 1535. An example of a manuscript chart on vellum produced during the period of Portuguese and Spanish imperial expansion. National flags indicate acknowledged spheres of influence.

usually assembled into large atlases, elegantly bound and often beautifully hand-coloured. Thanks to the purchases of Sir James Caird, the Museum possesses a large number of these magnificent volumes, representing nearly all the great Dutch publishers, such as Ortelius, Mercator, Waghenaer, Blaeu and Van Keulen.

But the seaman has been notoriously conservative throughout history and many navigators preferred to continue using the hand-drawn chart on vellum as being more robust and less vulnerable to damage by sea water. To satisfy this demand a group of English chartmakers flourished throughout the seventeenth century, concentrated in the narrow streets of Wapping and Radcliffe close by the Pool of London. Now known as the 'Thames School', they drew their charts to order, ingeniously illuminated on vellum and glued to hinged oak boards called 'platts'. The number of these attractive and interesting platts that survive in collections throughout the world bears witness to their durability, and the

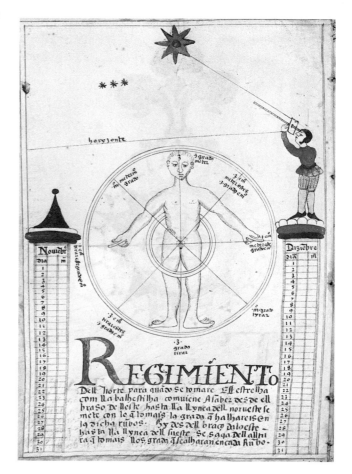

**The Rules of the North Star** from a Portuguese atlas, *c* 1555. The Portuguese and Spanish voyages of discovery depended for their success on the newly developed science of astronomic navigation. From this diagram the navigator could find the correction to apply to his observation of the height of the Pole Star to give him his true latitude.

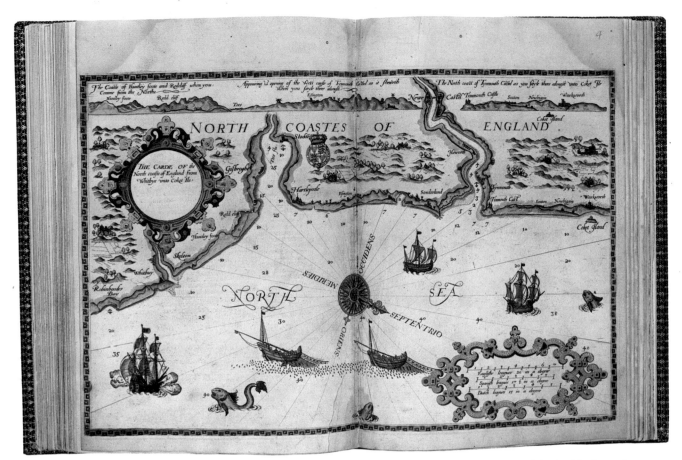

**Dutch chart of the north east coast of England** by Lucas Jansz Waghenaer, 1583. The Dutch master pilot Waghenaer produced the first comprehensive atlas of charts covering the coasts of Europe from the Baltic to Gibraltar. Called *De Spieghel der Zeevaerdt* (the Mariner's Mirror) it was translated into several European languages.

**Frontispiece from a Dutch sea atlas** by Pieter Goos, 1666.

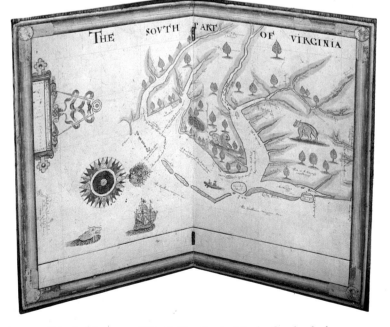

**'Platt' of the coast of North Carolina** by Nicolas Comberford, c 1657. This example of an English manuscript chart of the 'Thames School' shows clearly the method of mounting onto hinged oak boards. The area shown covers Pamlico and Albemarle Sounds together with Roanoke Island, the site of the first English colony in North America.

**The school of navigation** – detail from the frontispiece to a sea atlas by Jacob Colom, Amsterdam, 1663.

*Great Britain's Coasting Pilot* by Captain Greenvile Collins, 1693, the frontispiece.

seventeen in the Greenwich collection include several particularly fine examples.

The eighteenth century was a period of rapid advances in all the sciences, including hydrography. With the founding of the Académie Royale des Sciences in Paris in 1666 France took the lead in these advances, and her trained *ingenieurs hydrographes* retraced the coast of France and her overseas territories with the aid of new astronomic techniques and more accurate instruments.

In 1720, France established a central State hydrographic office for the express purpose of providing up-to-date charts to her navy. The first head of this office, and one of France's most famous hydrographers, was Jacques Nicholas Bellin. Through his exertions were produced the volumes of *Le Neptune François* and *Hydrographie Françoise*, containing charts for the whole world, strongly bound in leather for issue to all French men-of-war. This series was continued and expanded by his successors, culminating in the French *Neptune* of the early nineteenth century, comprising 435 charts in eleven volumes and combining in one superb set of engravings examples of the work of all the best hydrographers of the time.

Examples of these and all the most important works of hydrography produced during the period of French dominance are held in the collection. They include the Mediterranean port plans of the Royal pilot Jacques Ayrouard, Apres de Mannevillette's *Le Neptune Oriental* in several editions, and the charts produced by the important voyages of exploration of Bougainville, La Perouse, Dumont d'Urville and others.

Not surprisingly, it is in the field of British hydrography that the collections are strongest. After an initial flowering in Elizabethan times, when for a brief period

England led the world in navigational thought and practice, her influence declined and in the following centuries there were few English chartmakers to challenge the ascendancy of the Dutch, and later the French. The first English publisher to issue printed charts was John Seller. Although many of his charts were unashamed copies of Dutch originals, his *English Pilot* series of atlases, first published in 1671, faced little home competition and ran to many editions.

This unsatisfactory dependence on Dutch charts was recognized by Samuel Pepys, who in 1671, when Secretary to the Board of Admiralty, initiated the first organized hydrographic survey of British coastal waters. It was carried out by Captain Greenvile Collins, and the results, comprising forty-seven charts with accompanying sailing directions and tidal information, were published in 1691 as *Great Britain's Coasting Pilot*. Although criticized at the time for their lack of accuracy, the charts filled an urgent need, and over the next one hundred years the atlas ran to fourteen editions.

**Charlestown Harbour, South Carolina** from *The Atlantic Neptune* by J. F. W. DesBarres, 1776.

**Guayaquil, Ecuador.** A beautifully drawn chart by the Spanish cartographer Luis de Surville, 1778. He delighted in *trompe-l'œil* effects, such as the label in the left-hand corner.

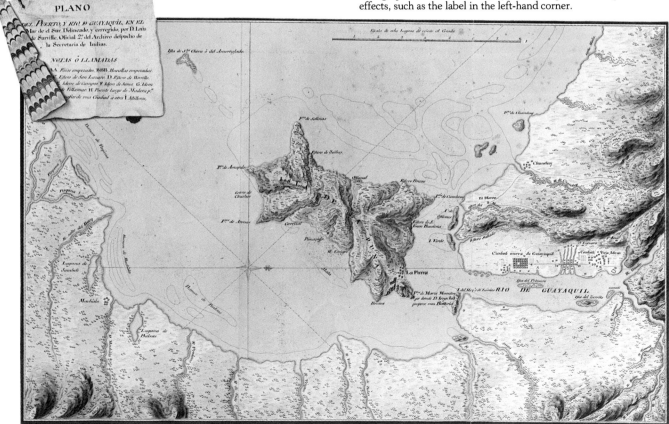

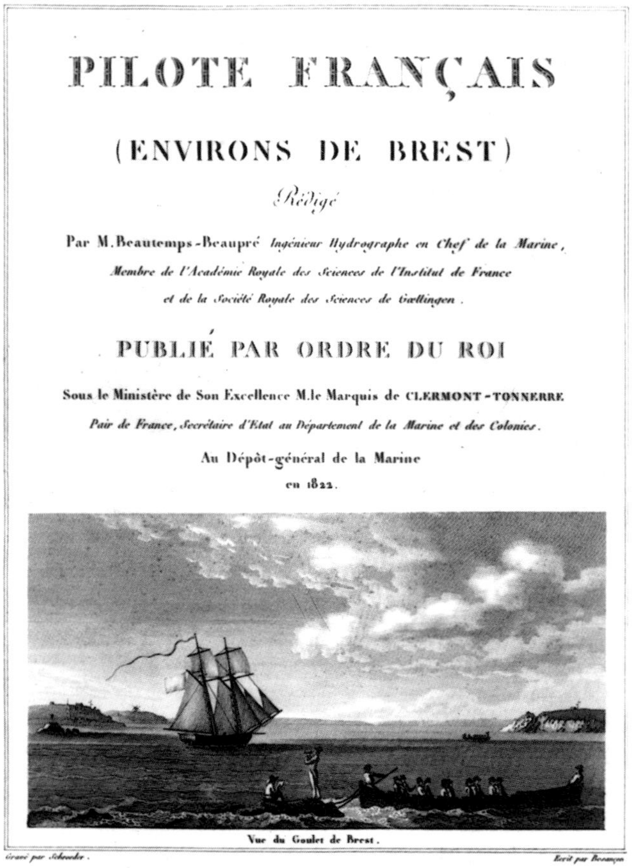
PILOTE FRANÇAIS

(ENVIRONS DE BREST)

Rédigé

Par M. Beautemps-Beaupré *Ingénieur Hydrographe en Chef de la Marine,*
*Membre de l'Académie Royale des Sciences de l'Institut de France*
*et de la Société Royale des Sciences de Gœttingen.*

PUBLIÉ PAR ORDRE DU ROI

Sous le Ministère de Son Excellence M. le Marquis de CLERMONT-TONNERRE
*Pair de France, Secrétaire d'Etat au Département de la Marine et des Colonies.*

Au Dépôt-général de la Marine
en 1822.

Vue du Goulet de Brest.

*Gravé par Schroeder.* *Ecrit par Besançon*

***Pilote Français*** by C. F. Beautemps-Beaupré, 1822, the title page. The *Pilote Français*, comprising 150 charts of the coast of France in six volumes, formed the culmination of the long and distinguished career of France's greatest hydrographer.

The development of hydrography in Britain was hampered by the reluctance of the Government to provide funds for organized surveys, and on the rare occasions when these took place they were usually under-financed. In the second half of the eighteenth century the failure of the fragmented commercial chart industry to provide adequate charts became increasingly apparent and attitudes began to change. Between 1740 and 1771 a civilian, Professor Murdoch Mackenzie, was employed by the Admiralty Board to make hydrographic surveys of the Orkneys, Ireland and the west coasts of Britain. Using much-improved instruments and the methods of triangulation developed in France, Mackenzie produced charts which set new standards of accuracy. These were published in 1776 in a two-volume atlas entitled *A maritim survey of Ireland and the West of Great Britain*, and in the same year he recorded his unrivalled surveying experience in a *Treatise on Maritim Surveying*, the first work in English devoted solely to the practice of hydrography.

Meanwhile the pace was quickening in Britain's growing territories overseas. In India and the East Indies the indefatigable Alexander Dalrymple, Hydrographer to the British East India Company, published over 400 charts and harbour plans derived from a wide variety of sources, including his own surveys. To the west, with the occupation of French Canada in 1763, the whole of North America came under British administration for a brief period, and an ambitious programme of hydrographic survey was launched under two army engineers, Captain Holland and Lieutenant DesBarres, and a naval master, James Cook, later to achieve fame as the Pacific explorer. These surveys resulted in the publication by DesBarres of the *Atlantic Neptune*, a superbly designed and lavishly produced series of 250 charts and views described at the time as 'one of the most remarkable products of human industry that has ever been given to the world through the arts of printing and engraving'. Examples of these charts can be admired in many institutions throughout the world, but the most definitive collection, comprising over 800 items, is preserved at Greenwich.

With the formation of the Hydrographic Office of the Admiralty in 1795, Great Britain belatedly adopted a policy which every maritime nation had found necessary since the Portuguese established their seaborne empire in the fifteenth century. Under the direction of a series of far-sighted hydrographers, and in response to the rapid increase of British shipping and trade, the scope and activities of the office expanded steadily throughout the nineteenth century. A professional surveying service was established, manned by officers from the fleet, and large areas of the globe owe their first accurate charts to British survey expeditions. In 1824 Admiralty charts, previously only issued to naval ships, were put on public sale and were soon in demand by shipping of all nations. By the end of the century the Admiralty were offering world-wide chart coverage with a total of 3089 charts. With few exceptions, the Admiralty chart collection at Greenwich contains copies of each new edition of every chart issued by the Hydrographic Department.

Taken together these collections form one of the most comprehensive and international on the subject of maritime cartography available to the public. Continually being augmented by gifts and purchases, they span 500 years of history.

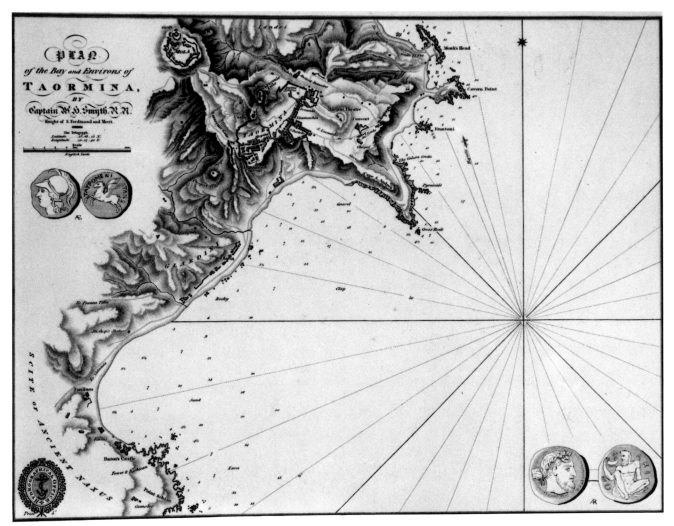

**Taormina, Sicily** by Captain W. H. Smyth, 1823. This example of an early production of the Admiralty hydrographic office shows the high standard of copper engraving reached in the nineteenth century.

---

## The Navigation Collection

### ALAN STIMSON
*Curator of Navigation and Deputy Head
of the Department of Navigation and Astronomy*

**Sixteenth century navigational instruments.** Mariner's astrolabe for measuring the height of the Sun above the horizon in order to find the latitude (*left*), probably Spanish *c* 1585; rare ivory Mariner's compass (*top*), probably Italian *c* 1570; brass mounted lodestone used to restore the magnetism of soft iron compass needles, current in the sixteenth century (*right*).

**Two sixteenth-century surveying instruments:** the first English theodolite, inscribed *H. Cole 1574*, made to the design of Leonard Digges and described in his *Pantometria* of 1571 (*left*); Pierre Danfries' graphometer, *c* 1600 contrasted with the illustration in his book describing its use which was published in Paris in 1597 (*right*).

It is a remarkable fact that a museum which first opened its doors as recently as 1937 should have such a large and representative collection of navigational and scientific instruments. The nucleus of the collections was presented to the Museum by its greatest benefactor Sir James Caird in the 1930s and 40s, when many instruments were bought through dealers in Paris and London. The collections have grown at a steady rate since those times with the largest addition in 1969, when the Admiralty Compass Observatory transferred its entire collection of over 3000 magnetic compasses, binnacles and associated items to the Museum.

Collecting policies have changed in recent years, and whereas early efforts were directed towards eighteenth- and nineteenth-century instruments, these are now added to only in exceptional circumstances. More energy is being directed towards building up a comprehensive collection of electronic and radio aids to navigation, and the scope of the collection has been widened to include the subjects of marine meteorology and oceanography.

The collection has always included a number of instruments of a non-marine nature (a legacy of indiscriminate bulk-buying in the 1930s), but it can generally be described under four main heads – navigational, surveying, oceanographical and meteorological. It is not possible to display all the nearly 6000 items in the collection, so a large part is held in reserve where it is available for study and for loan to other museums and exhibitions.

**A case of silver drawing instruments** inscribed on the parallel rule *Made by Tho Wright Instrument maker to his* MAJESTY, *c* 1730. The case contains the instruments of a military surveyor who would have used them for artillery calculations and drawing plans of fortifications and surveys.

Navigation as a professional skill can be said to have developed in classical times in the almost tideless waters of the Mediterranean and was based on *direction*, found from the position of the sun and stars or prevailing wind direction, and *estimated distance*, based upon the sailing or rowing speed of the ship.

In the unpredictable weather of northern waters different techniques were required to combat the fierce currents and rise and fall of the tides. The shallow waters of the continental shelf demanded skill in interpreting the depth of water and recognizing the rocks and proliferating shoals around these shores, and bred an altogether different type of seaman.

The first improvement to both these largely innate skills, requiring more than a sounding lead and line or a sense of direction, was the invention of the magnetic compass in the Mediterranean sometime in the twelfth century. At the same time sea charts drawn on vellum began to appear. No major navigational improvements followed until the Portuguese and Spanish voyages of exploration in the fifteenth and sixteenth centuries created a need for more accurate methods of recording the extent of their discoveries. Methods of finding latitude (distance north or south of the equator) were evolved by scientists ashore, together with instruments with which to measure the altitude of the sun or a star, as well as tables of astronomical data.

The new skills were gradually introduced to northern seamen by translations of navigation text books such as Pedro Medina's *Art de Navegar* published in 1545 and first translated into English in 1581, and also by instruction from trained Portuguese and Spanish navigators such as Sebastian Cabot (1476–1557). Surviving instruments from this period are rare and the Museum is fortunate to have a fine brass mariner's astrolabe, an Italian compass and several lodestones which can be dated to before 1600.

The sixteenth century also saw the increasing use of mathematics and geometry, and what was once regarded as a 'black art' became increasingly useful in laying out fortifications, in gunnery, and in surveying towns and estates. Of the many ingenious instruments in the collection produced at this time, perhaps the most important is the theodolite, an English invention, described by Leonard Digges in his *Pantometria* of 1571. The Museum's instrument was made by Humphrey Cole in 1574 and is the earliest surviving example.

Although English navigators had used the cross-staff since the mid-sixteenth century, and Captain John Davies's backstaff since its invention in 1594 to measure star and sun altitudes, examples of neither instrument

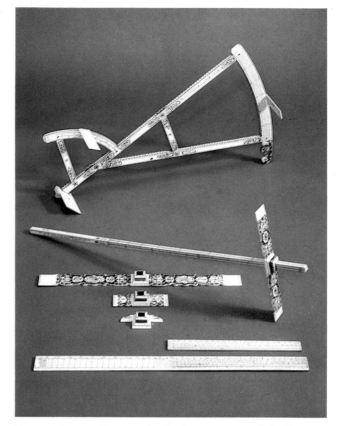

**Presentation set of ivory navigation instruments** made by Thomas Tuttell of Charing Cross, London *c* 1700. (*From top to bottom*): a Davis quadrant or backstaff used to measure the Sun's height above the horizon; a cross staff with 90, 60, 30 and 10 degree crosses used to measure the height of the Sun or a star above the horizon; two Gunter's scales, forerunners of the modern slide rule, with which trigonometrical nautical problems could be solved.

appear in the Museum's collection earlier than the non-typical but magnificent ivory presentation set made by Thomas Tuttell in 1700. In fact very few wooden instruments before this date have survived anywhere, apart from some examples of Gunter's rule and the sector, both precursors of the slide-rule calculator.

The seventeenth-century navigator continued to use the methods and instruments of the previous century, but much effort both ashore and afloat was expended on the apparently insoluble problem of how to find longitude (distance east or west measured on the Earth's surface) at sea. It had been appreciated since the early sixteenth century that the answer lay in the ability to calculate the time of day at the ship and at a standard place at the same moment.

In England the formation of the Royal Society in 1661 was part of a national expanding scientific awareness. In 1675 the Royal Observatory was built at Greenwich and John Flamsteed, the first Astronomer Royal, was instructed to apply himself to solving the longitude problem. However, a solution was not reached until the middle of the eighteenth century, despite a prize of

**Early eighteenth-century navigation instruments.** Hadley octant stamped GEO. ADAMS LONDON, FECIT 1753, used for measuring the height above the horizon of the Sun or a star and gradually adopted by seamen in preference to the backstaff and cross-staff (*left*); azimuth compass inscribed *J. Fowler London*, *c* 1700, used to find magnetic variation, the difference between true north and magnetic north (*centre*); improved backstaff fitted with a lens to focus the Sun's rays stamped *Made by Will Garner for Oliver Thompson 1734* (*right*).

£20,000 offered by Parliament in 1714 to stimulate further endeavour. One early solution, much favoured by the astronomers, lay in using the Moon as an astronomical clock as it moved against the background of stars. Another involved constructing a clock that would keep time in a rolling ship at sea despite variations in temperature and the effects of poor lubrication. Both methods required a more sophisticated instrument to measure the necessary astronomical observations than was then available.

A country gentleman and amateur scientist, John Hadley, provided the solution to the observing instrument problem when he described his newly invented reflecting octant to the Royal Society in 1731. Hadley's Quadrant (as seamen called it) enabled accurate measurements to be made for the first time from the deck of a ship. The 'rightness' of the original design enabled it to be developed into the sextant by about 1757, and it continues in use in modified form to the present day. The Museum can boast perhaps the world's most comprehensive collection of Hadley octants, sextants and reflecting circles, possessing over 230 instruments dating from the original commercial form of the instrument of about 1740 to examples of sextants made only a few years ago.

**Late eighteenth-century navigation instruments.** Hadley octant by an English maker, 1770 (*left*); azimuth compass inscribed *Invented and made by Rust and Eyre in ye Minories London*, *c* 1770 (*centre*); pillar-framed sextant inscribed *Ramsden London*, 1798 (*right*).

**John Harrison's first marine timekeeper for finding the longitude, 1735.** This large clock was fitted with a temperature compensation device, a novel escapement known as a 'grasshopper', and was almost frictionless in operation.

Both longitude theories were made practicable within a few years of each other; by the Yorkshire carpenter and self-taught clockmaker John Harrison, whose series of timekeepers culminated in his prize-winning watch H.4. in 1759, and by the annual publication by the Astronomer Royal of lunar prediction tables in the *Nautical Almanac* beginning in the year 1767. Captain James Cook proved the efficacy of the new methods during his great voyages of discovery between 1769 and 1780.

**Larcum Kendall's copy of John Harrison's fourth marine timekeeper, known as K1, 1769.** This large watch of just over five inches diameter successfully completed two voyages with Captain James Cook.

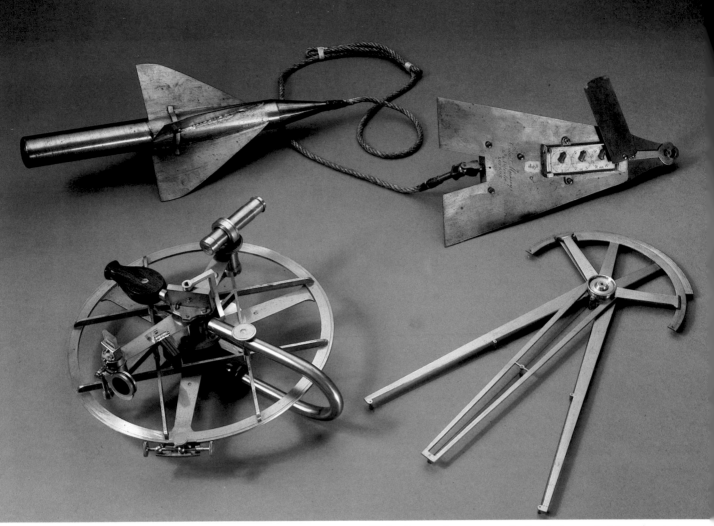

**Early nineteenth-century navigation instruments.** Massey's patent ship's log, *c* 1830 (*top*) – Edward Massey invented the first commercially successful distance recorder in 1802. Reflecting circle inscribed *Troughton London. c* 1800 (*left*), used to measure the distance between the moon and certain stars in the 'luner distance' method of finding longitude. Station pointer inscribed *Troughton London, c* 1820 (*right*), used to plot a ship's position on a chart from the bearings of distant objects.

The London instrument makers responded to the new demand by producing improved chronometers and sextants as well as all types of mathematical, optical and philosophical instruments. Improved technology had already resulted in John Dollond's colour-free achromatic telescopes in 1755 and the superior magnetic compasses of Dr Gowin Knight. Between 1768 and 1773 Jesse Ramsden developed his scale-dividing machine, which enabled smaller and more accurate instruments to be made. Edward Troughton patented his pillar-frame sextant in 1788, and Edward Masey his mechanical ship's log for recording distance sailed in 1802. Improvements in quality to all types of instrument were achieved, and many London instrument and chronometer makers acquired international reputations.

The navigation collection is particularly rich in objects from this period, and the Navigation Room displays many of the inventions mentioned. Pride of place goes to

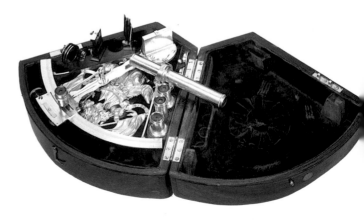

**King Edward VII's silver sextant** presented when he was Prince of Wales. Inscribed *Mrs Janet Taylor, 104 Minories, London, c* 1855. Mrs Taylor ran a navigation school and instrument making business for over thirty years and exhibited at the Great Exhibition of 1851.

the Harrison timekeepers and the chronometers used by Captain Cook and Captain Bligh which can be seen – and heard – ticking off the seconds more than 200 years after they were first set going.

Refinements of the new navigational techniques and improvements to existing instruments continued in the nineteenth century, although the many small instrument-making firms gradually evolved into fewer, larger businesses whose products became more utilitarian in appearance; embellishment and polished brass were not economic.

The emphasis now moved to developing a magnetic compass that would operate successfully in an iron or steel ship. This was not achieved until Sir William Thomson (later Lord Kelvin) combined all the necessary corrections and improvements in one binnacle which he patented in 1876.

The many prototypes and designs of compass and binnacle in the Admiralty Compass Observatory collection of magnetic compasses effectively tell the story of the attempt during the nineteenth century to produce an efficient compass. Ironically, with the early twentieth-century development of the gyroscopic compass the

**Sir William Thomson compass and binnacle,** *c* 1882. Sir William Thomson, later Lord Kelvin, designed in 1876 the first successfully compensated magnetic compass for use in iron ships.

**The oldest dated telescope in the collection.** Stamped IACOB CUNIGHAM 1661 on the object lens cap. The barrel of the telescope is of leather-covered wood, while the draw tubes are of card covered in marbled paper. It magnifies about three times.

**Combined telescope and watch** believed to have been presented by Lord Macartney to the Emperor Chien-lung on 14 September 1793 during his Embassy to China. It is inscribed *Frazer & Son, London*; the watch is probably French.

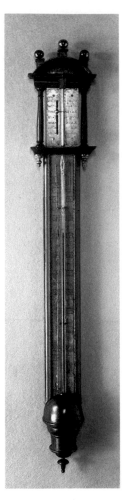

**Domestic barometer and thermometer,** *c*1710 inscribed I. PATRICK LONDON. Mercury barometers became popular for 'telling the weather' at the end of the seventeenth century. The thermometer has the original Royal Society scale graduated from Extreme cold (90°) to Blood heat (0°).

**Theodolites:** theodolite fitted with telescopic sights and rackwork movement of the vertical and horizontal circles inscribed *J. Sisson London*, 1737 (*left*); theodolite with telescopic sights and Ramsden's auxiliary telescope inscribed *Dollond London*, 1840 (*right*).

magnetic compass has become a backup system except for its use in smaller craft. Very little of the Museum's twentieth-century radio and electronic equipment is on display in the galleries, chiefly because much of it requires careful cleaning and restoration, although the first commercial radar fitted in the merchant ship S.S. *Birdwood* in 1949 can be seen in Neptune Hall.

The modern navigator is increasingly reliant on electronic technology, with the expansion of such aids as the Decca navigator and satellite navigation, so that the modern versions of Hadley's octant and Harrison's timekeepers are becoming less important. Whether it will be possible to display the products of modern technology in as pleasing a fashion as the instruments of the previous centuries remains to be seen.

**Marine radar type 159, 1949.** This radar display unit is one of six pre-production prototypes fitted in 1949 to ships engaged in the coastal and short seas trade. This particular unit was fitted in the collier SS *Birdwood*.

# Astronomy and Time

DEREK HOWSE
*Head of the Department of Navigation and Astronomy*

**King Charles II,** founder of the Royal Observatory.
Miniature by Samuel Cooper, *c* 1665.

The collections held by the National Maritime Museum covering the history of astronomy and time are world-famous. They include marine chronometers, precision clocks and watches, astrolabes and other models of the heavens, hour glasses and sundials, portable telescopes and many important printed books and manuscripts on these subjects. Undoubtedly, the most important of the astronomy collections in the Museum is that in the Old Royal Observatory on Observatory Hill, whose buildings were progressively transferred to the National Maritime Museum in the 1950s when the astronomers forsook smoky Greenwich for the clearer skies of Sussex.

## Greenwich Observatory

In the seventeenth century one of the most vital scientific problems demanding a solution was that of discovering the longitude. It was specifically to provide the data to achieve this that King Charles II was persuaded to found his own Royal Observatory at Greenwich in 1675.

Economy was the order of the day. Built on the foundations of the tower built by Humphrey of Glouces-

**The Royal Observatory** immediately after completion, *c* 1676. The Queen's House can be seen (*left*), at the bottom of the hill.

PROSPECTUS  SEPTENTRIONALIS.

**The 'Great Room'** of the observatory, central feature of Christopher Wren's design for the Astronomer Royal's residence. Today the building is called Flamsteed House, and the room itself the Octagon Room.

ter, using second-hand bricks from Tilbury Fort and wood, iron and lead from a demolished gatehouse at the Tower of London, Sir Christopher Wren, assisted by that versatile architect-scientist Robert Hooke, arranged for the building of what is today known as Flamsteed House. John Flamsteed, the King's 'observator', moved into the building now called after him on 10 July 1676.

The buildings were progressively extended eastward and southward by successive Astronomers Royal to accommodate additional instruments and staff – Halley's Quadrant House in 1725, Bradley's New Observatory in 1749, Maskelyne's terrace observatories in 1773, Pond's Circle Room in 1809 and East Building in 1813, Airy's Magnetic Observatory in 1837, his fireproof record rooms in 1854, his Great Equatorial Building in 1857 and his new library in 1881. And during this time and later, existing buildings were being continually modified.

For the first 200 years of its existence, the work of the observatory was almost exclusively related to the needs of navigation, though the by-products – for example, the Greenwich Meridian and the world's time-zone system

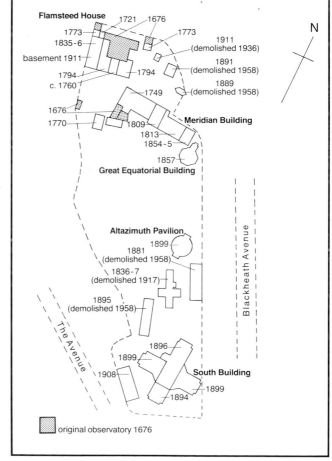

**The Observatory buildings, 1675–1960.**

based on it – were of tremendous value to those ashore and in astronomy generally. In the nineteenth century, however, developments in photography and spectroscopy gave rise to the new science of astrophysics, the study of what Sun, Moon and stars are made of, how they are born and how they die. Christie's New Physical Observatory (today's South Building), surmounted by the Thompson 30-inch and 26-inch photographic telescopes, was finished in 1899 expressly for the study of this new subject. Christie's Altazimuth Pavilion on the main site and a new Magnetic Observatory in an enclosure in the Park (now demolished), a quarter of a mile to the east, were also completed in 1899. The last major astronomical building work at Greenwich took place under Dyson's superintendence, when domes for two telescopes were erected in the Christie enclosure in 1932, the magnetic observatory having moved to Abinger in Surrey in 1923.

By the 1930s the smoke and street lights of metropolitan London had made Greenwich Park no longer a fit place for England's premier observatory and a search for a new site was started. Owing to the War, it was not until 1945 that the decision was taken to move to Herstmonceux Castle near Eastbourne in Sussex, and not until 1956 that the move was completed and all the old buildings handed over to the National Maritime Museum.

Prince Philip (one of the Museum's Trustees) opened the Octagon Room to the public in May 1953 and the Queen opened the whole of Flamsteed House in July 1960. Prince Philip then opened the Greenwich Planetarium in the South Building in November 1965 and Sir Richard Woolley, eleventh Astronomer Royal, opened Flamsteed's observatory and the Meridian Building in July 1967. In May 1975, the Queen paid a return visit to mark the three-hundredth anniversary of the foundation of the Royal Observatory, seeing the restored 28-inch telescope as a working instrument in the Great Equatorial Building.

### The Old Royal Observatory today

The contents of the buildings can be best described by taking an imaginary tour following the route recommended for the Museum's visitors. It starts in Greenwich Park outside the Observatory gates not far from General Wolfe's statue with its incomparable view of the Museum's Main Buildings and London beyond. Looking west towards Flamsteed House we are immediately reminded why the name Greenwich is so well-known the world over: on the eastern turret of Flamsteed House is the red Time ball, the world's first visual time signal,

The **Shepherd 24-hour clock** (*foreground*), erected outside the gates in 1852, the year the Greenwich Time Service started sending time signals to every place then connected to London by electric telegraph. **Flamsteed House** (*background*) with the **Time Ball** on the staff on the roof: except during the War years, the ball has dropped at precisely 1 p.m. daily since 1833.

which since 1833 has been hoisted half-way up the mast at 12.55, to the top at 12.58, and dropped at precisely 13.00 – not at noon, because at that time the astronomers were busy observing the Sun's passage across the meridian, in effect actually finding the time. Also seen from the Park is the 24-hour Gate Clock in the Observatory wall. Entering the courtyard with Flamsteed House ahead of us and the Meridian Building on our left, we cross a brass line on the ground which marks the Greenwich Meridian, chosen in 1884 as the world's Prime Meridian – longitude zero.

We enter Flamsteed House and immediately turn right up the seventeenth-century staircase to the Octagon Room, one of the few Christopher Wren interiors to have survived virtually unchanged. Down the stairs on the west side of the Octagon Room, we come to the rooms, the first of which is known as Edmond Halley Gallery, built on the south side of the house in the eighteenth and early nineteenth centuries. In these rooms the theme, broadly speaking, is 'Time'.

'THAT THE CONFERENCE PROPOSES TO THE GOVERNMENTS HERE REPRESENTED THE ADOPTION OF THE MERIDIAN PASSING THROUGH THE CENTRE OF THE TRANSIT INSTRUMENT AT THE OBSERVATORY OF GREENWICH AS THE INITIAL MERIDIAN FOR LONGITUDE' (Resolution II of the International Meridian Conference, Washington, DC, October 1884). The telescope defining the meridian can be seen (*centre*).

**Greenwich meridian.** Being photographed on the Meridian is almost obligatory for the many thousands of tourists and school children who visit the Old Royal Observatory every year.

The first thing we see in Halley Gallery is a display of planispheric astrolabes, said to be the second largest collection in the world. With this very versatile instrument – probably a Greek invention of about the second century BC – one can find the positions of the Sun and stars for any time and date, or conversely, find the time of day by measuring the position of a particular star in the sky, or find the times of sunrise and sunset, the height of a building, the depth of a well, the direction of Mecca, and so on. Also in Halley Gallery is the greater part of the Museum's superb collection of examples of other models of the heavens such as armillary spheres, orreries and planetaria, ranging in date from 1230 to 1900. One of the many interesting exhibits is the exquisite table clock made for King Casimir V of Poland by Caspar Buschmann of Augsberg in about 1586, which has no less than eleven dials showing not only the hour and minute but the date, the day of the week, feasts and saints' days, the Golden Number, Epact and Dominical Letter of the current year and times of sunrise and sunset. It also has a clockwork astrolabe showing the current positions of the brightest stars. It strikes the hours and quarters and has an alarum facility, and there is also a removable dial-plate incorporating a magnetic compass and four different varieties of sundial.

The next room is Nevil Maskelyne Gallery, named after the fifth Astronomer Royal, who lived here from 1765 until his death in 1811 and who had this room built in 1790. It is devoted mostly to sundials, fixed and portable, with globes to provide visual interest. Some of the dials near the windows actually tell the time when the sun shines. In the showcase entitled 'Compendia' is an exquisite pocket instrument made by the eminent English instrument maker Humphrey Cole in 1569, and at one time said, probably erroneously, to have belonged to Sir Francis Drake. Just 6.3 cm (2.5 in) in diameter, it opens up in four leaves incorporating a sundial, a compass, a nocturnal and a geometrical square (for measuring heights and distances of buildings); it also records the latitudes of cities, tidal information, movable feasts and positions and phases of the Moon.

The Nathaniel Bliss Gallery, with its exhibits of hour glasses and nocturnals (for telling the time at night by measuring the angle of the Plough relative to the Pole star), completes the display of non-mechanical time-telling devices.

Downstairs in Spencer Jones Gallery, named after the last Astronomer Royal to live in this house (from 1933–48), we come to what might be called 'time which ticks' – mechanical clocks and watches. The main interest here is in precision timekeepers, covering not only the

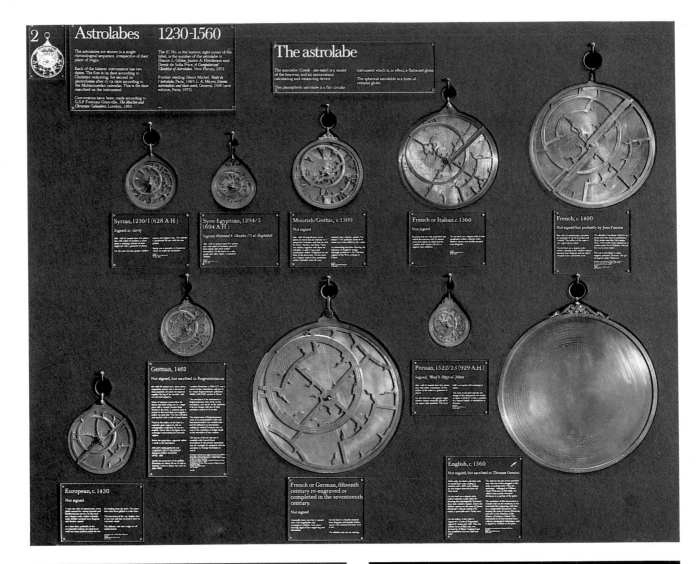

# Astrolabes 1230-1560

The astrolabes are shown in a single chronological sequence, irrespective of their place of origin.

Each of the Islamic instruments has two dates. The first is its date according to Christian reckoning, the second (in parentheses after it) its date according to the Mohammedan calendar. This is the date inscribed on the instrument.

Conversions have been made according to G.S.P. Freeman-Grenville, *The Muslim and Christian Calendars*, London, 1963.

The IC No. in the bottom right corner of the label, is the number of the astrolabe in Sharon L. Gibbs, Janice A. Henderson and Derek de Solla Price, *A Computerized Checklist of Astrolabes*, New Haven, 1973.

Further reading: Henri Michel, *Traité de l'astrolabe*, Paris, 1947; L. A. Mayer, *Islamic astrolabists and their work*, Geneva, 1956 (new edition, Paris, 1975).

## The astrolabe

The astrolabe (Greek - *star-take*) is a model of the heavens, and an astronomical calculating and measuring device.

The planispheric astrolabe is a flat circular instrument which is, in effect, a flattened globe.

The spherical astrolabe is a form of celestial globe.

Syrian, 1230/1 (628 A.H.)
Signed: *as-Sarraj*

Syro-Egyptian, 1294/5 (694 A.H.)
Signed: Mahmud b. Shuaika (?) al-Baghdadi

Moorish/Gothic, c.1300
Not signed

French or Italian c. 1360
Not signed

French, c. 1400
Not signed but probably by Jean Fusoris

German, 1462
Not signed, but ascribed to Regiomontanus

Persian, 1522/23 (929 A.H.)
Signed, *'Abd'a Hajji al-Jilani*

European, c. 1430
Not signed

French or German, fifteenth century re-engraved or completed in the seventeenth century.
Not signed

English, c. 1560
Not signed, but ascribed to Thomas Gemini

△ **Time-telling without clocks** (*left to right*): 15-minute sandglass, probably English, sixteenth century; nocturnal, boxwood, signed *J[ohn] B[rowne]*, English, c 1660; horizontal garden sundial, brass, signed *Elias Allen fecit*, English, c 1635; mechanical equinoctial sundial, brass, signed *Wm* DEANE *Fecit in Crane Court, Fleet Street*, LONDON, c 1690; portable polyhedral sundial, ivory, English, eighteenth century.

**Seventeenth and eighteenth century universal ring sundials** in Nevil Maskelyne Gallery. Folding up flat for transport, these can be used to tell the time anywhere in the world, on land or at sea. Most of these dials were used suspended from the hand. The one at bottom left was designed to be used on a flat surface, giving potentially greater accuracy.

▷

**Models of the heavens** (*left to right*): celestial globe, glass, enclosing a planetarium, French, *c* 1790; earth-centred armillary sphere, brass, signed MACQUART À PARIS, *c* 1730; portable orrery, wood and paper with brass fittings, signed *W & S Jones . . . London*, probably *c* 1810; sun-centred armillary sphere, iron, probably sixteenth century.

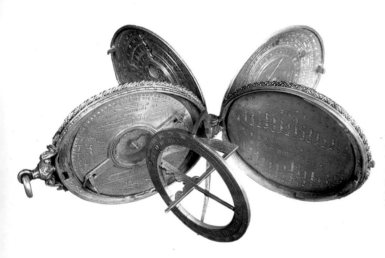

**So-called 'Drake's Dial'.** Pocket compendium, signed *Humfray Colle made this diall anno 1569*, described in the text. The opening facing the camera gives the means of finding the time by the Sun and of observing vertical or horizontal angles, and includes a compass; the right-hand opening gives a perpetual calendar and lunar aspects and phases; the left-hand opening gives the means of finding the times of the tides for 80 ports in north-west Europe.

development of the marine chronometer, but also astronomers' clocks, particularly those used at Greenwich. The story of the spread of Greenwich Time is told from its beginning in the seventeenth century, when it was of interest only to the two astronomers living here, to the present day, when it is the basis of time kept the world over. Examples can be seen – most of them ticking away – of many of the clocks used to find and distribute Greenwich Time over the last 200 years. Particularly interesting is the Shepherd electric clock which controlled the first Greenwich time service (and the Observatory Time ball and Gate Clock) from 1852, automatically dropping a Time ball at Deal seventy miles away by electric telegraph as early as 1854.

Upstairs and on the way out of Flamsteed House, we pass through the seventeenth-century rooms furnished in contemporary style but not, alas, with Flamsteed's original furniture. A walk across the courtyard and through the upper garden leads into Flamsteed's Observatory, the rooms at the bottom of the garden where most of his serious astronomy was done. Although Flamsteed was paid £100 a year and given a house to live in, he had to provide all his own instruments so, after his death and despite threats of legal action from the

Government, his widow removed them. Except for three Tompion clocks they have never been seen since, which means that all we can show today are full-sized models of the foundation equipment, albeit in their original positions.

After Flamsteed, the Government changed its policy and paid for the instruments – the majority of which survive and can be seen in their working settings in the Meridian Building. The first room is the Quadrant Room in which the 1725 meridian wall of Edmond Halley (of comet fame) is still standing with two great 8 ft mural quadrants mounted on it. This room was incorporated in Bradley's new observatory of 1749, the Quadrant House to the west housing the meridian quadrants for measuring the vertical positions of the heavenly bodies (polar distances), and the Transit Room to the east with the transit instrument for measuring the horizontal positions (right ascensions). In the centre was the accommodation for the Astronomer Royal's assistant, with a bedroom upstairs and a library and study downstairs. Bradley's transit room is of particular interest because the Greenwich Meridian used in Britain's first official maps – the Ordnance Survey of 1787 – passed through it.

**Astronomical table clock,** signed CASPAR BVSCHMAN [Augsburg], c 1586, described in the text. The top dial shows the time of day, the date by both Julian and Gregorian calendars, the Sun's position in the Zodiac, Saints' days, the Moon's age, phase and aspect, and the position of the Sun and 29 brightest stars. The dial on the left-hand face shows the day of the week; the other two dials show the length of the day, the times of sunrise and sunset, and the Sun's position in the zodiac. That a clock should give so much information was characteristic of German clockmaking of the period.

One of the seventeenth-century rooms in Flamsteed House

**Marine Chronometers:** 8-day, signed *Howells and Pennington* FOR *Thos Mudge No. 4. c* 1795 (*left*); 1-day, signed *John Arnold & Son London Inv et Fecit No. 23,* (*top centre*); chronometer watch, signed J B DENT & *Sons 9268.* Hall Mark 1892 (*bottom centre*); 1-day, signed *Thos Earnshaw* INVᵗ ET FECIT *No. 512 London 2856* (*right*).

**Airy's Transit Circle of 1852,** whose optical axis defines the
Greenwich Meridian.

Next to Bradley's transit room is Airy's transit circle room, converted from Pond's circle room in 1850 to accommodate Airy's new transit circle whose optical axis was chosen, by international agreement in 1884, to define the world's prime meridian, still the basis for time kept the world over.

Whereas most of the Meridian Building has been restored to its original appearance, with telescopes in their working positions, the rooms at the east end of the building (added in 1813 as staff accommodation) have been converted into conventional museum galleries with showcases and free-standing telescopes and clocks not necessarily in their original working settings. Downstairs is John Pond Gallery, containing a variety of nineteenth-century astronomical apparatus used at Greenwich or on expeditions such as those to observe the Transits of Venus in 1874 and 1882. Upstairs is Frank Dyson Gallery, devoted first to the display of the Sir William Herschel collection of telescopes and apparatus, used by the famous organist-turned-astronomer who discovered the planet Uranus in 1781. In 1789 he erected at Slough his great 40 ft reflecting telescope, which remained the world's largest telescope for fifty years. One of its objective mirrors, 121 cm (48 in) in diameter, is on display adjacent to an exquisite model which shows how the telescope looked in its heyday. Dominating the centre of the room is the 6 m long (20 ft) telescope tube made for Herschel in 1783 and taken to South Africa in 1834 by his son John for the survey of the southern skies. The remainder of the room is devoted to the work of the Royal Observatory over the last 300 years, not only in astronomy but also in magnetism and meteorology.

## Other buildings

The Old Royal Observatory has other buildings not open to the general public: the Great Equatorial Building surmounted by the Onion Dome with the 28-in refracting telescope of 1893 mounted and in full working order and available for use by astronomers, professional or

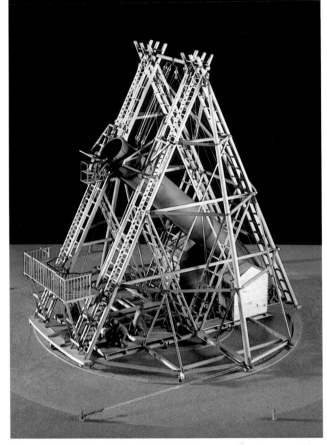

**A model of William Herschel's 40 ft telescope.** The observer sits on a platform with his eyepiece in the mouth of the tube. One of the original 48 ft objective mirrors can be seen today in Frank Dyson Gallery, near this model.

**The 28-inch refracting telescope** by Grubb of Dublin, which in 1893 replaced the 13-inch Merz Great Equatorial Refractor of 1859. Because the new telescope was 10 feet longer than the old one, the original drum-shaped dome had to be replaced by the familiar 'onion dome'. The telescope and its mounting were moved to the Royal Greenwich Observatory, Herstmonceaux, in 1947, returning to Greenwich in 1971. Because of extensive air-raid damage in the Second World War, the original *papier-mâché*-covered dome was demolished in 1953 and a new one of the same appearance but modern materials was constructed in 1974.

**Replica of one of the tent observatories** taken by Captain Cook on his third voyage of exploration 1776–9, erected ashore whenever the ships stayed in one place for any length of time, to determine accurate geographical positions and to check the going of the chronometers. The regulator clock by Shelton (*left*) and 12-inch astronomical quadrant by Bird (*right*) both sailed with Cook on one or more of his voyages. The 2 ft focus Gregorian telescope by Watkins (*centre*) is similar to those he carried.

**Instruments from the Barberini Collection** in the Queen's House.

amateur; the Altazimuth Pavilion, which contains a 16 cm refractor with a 10 cm photoheliograph on the same mounting, both in working order; and the South Building, which houses the Greenwich Planetarium and other offices.

### Astronomy in the Museum's Main Buildings

The collection of marine chronometers is large enough to allow for displays covering two different aspects of the subject: the chronometer as a piece of precision clock-work in the Spencer Jones Gallery of the Old Royal Observatory, and the chronometer as a navigational instrument in the Navigation Room at the bottom of the hill, where the displays of early chronometers are dominated by those of John 'Longitude' Harrison. All working, they include his famous No. 4, which in 1773 won the £20,000 award under Queen Anne's Longitude Act of 1714, together with Larcum Kendall's copy of No. 4, carried by Captain Cook on his last two voyages of exploration, and which Cook described as 'our faithful guide through all the vicissitudes of climates'. In the Cook Gallery are some of the original astronomical instruments and clocks used on his voyages.

**Galileo Galilei (1564–1642),** often described as the first man to use a telescope for astronomical purposes. Cardinal Barberini was one of those who spoke up for Galileo at the latter's trial before the Inquisition in Rome in 1633 for his heresy in declaring that the Earth was not the centre of the universe. Reliquary bust carved in pearwood, Italian *c* 1650–70, formerly in the Methuen Collection.

Finally, in the south-east room of the ground floor of the Queen's House is displayed the Barberini Collection of scientific instruments. Said to have been assembled by Cardinal Francesco Barberini (1597–1679), nephew of Pope Urban VIII, it provides an excellent example of the cabinets of aristocratic collectors and patrons of science in the seventeenth century.

# Printed Books and Manuscripts

DAVID PROCTOR
*Head of the Department of Printed Books & Manuscripts*

From early times a sea captain was obliged to maintain accurate records of his ship and her voyages, to help him account to the owners for her safety, equipment and profitability. The owners would probably include members of his home community, himself and even some of his crew. Today, of course, ships are extremely costly capital ventures and they are usually owned by large and highly organized chartered companies. Official regulations require records to be kept, so it is still an essential part of any captain's daily life to write up the ship's log and to check other papers, such as cargo, passenger and crew lists and equipment records.

In a modern ship, specialist officers keep separate lists and logs of the engines and of fittings such as wireless and radar equipment. The captain and navigating

officers may also keep personal navigational records of hazards and safe anchorages, although with the advent of technological aids this kind of record has become far less necessary than in the past, when personal knowledge of weather, wind, currents and coastlines was vital. The captain of an eighteenth-century merchant ship was out of touch with owners for many months and had to depend on his own initiative and knowledge to take decisions about cargoes and destinations. Records formed the essential proof of his ability or otherwise to make the ship pay a profit. In the case of warships, the

**Woodcut map of the world** by Ptolemy (*c* AD 150), published in Ulm, 1482. Note the names and personifications of the winds on the border and the system of latitude and longitude devised by Ptolemy for drawing maps.

captain and the admiral had to show that the ship and fleet were properly manned, equipped and capable of winning a battle.

Although seamen were not usually considered to have great literary skills, there can be few professions where so much written evidence of life and habits survives. Many of the officers who served in sailing ships had the time and inclination, or were in some cases obliged as part of their training, to keep personal illustrated logs or journals. Today, with the greatly increased speed of ships and shorter turn-round in harbour, there is far less opportunity for this kind of record-keeping. Until the twentieth century, virtually all these records were in manuscript and even today the law requires that basic records are still kept in this way.

For the ordinary passengers, a sea voyage was often a great and unusual experience and many recorded this in private journals and letters. Some were embellished with

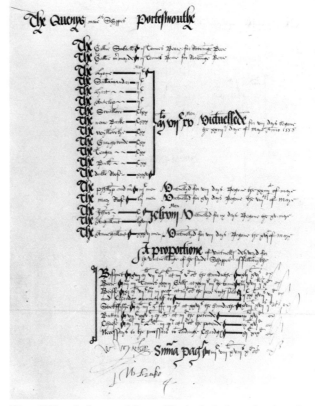

**List of Victuals** for one of Queen Elizabeth I's ships, dated 1558 and signed by Sir W. Wynter and William Broke.

**Copper engraved map of the world** by Abraham Ortelius from his atlas, published in Antwerp, 1570. Comparison with the Ptolemy map demonstrates how much has changed, following the great voyages of discovery.

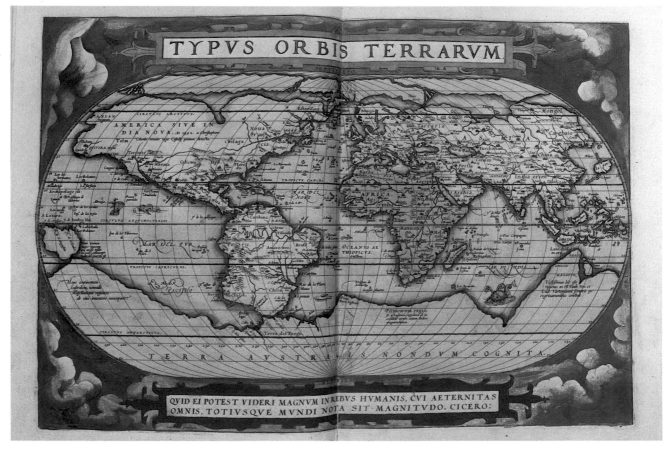

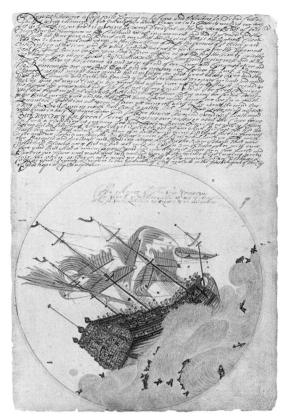

**The *Joseph Sampson*** in a gale, from the Journal of his sea voyages 1659–1703, kept by Edward Barlow (b. 1642).

**Song composed by Queen Elizabeth I** to commemorate the defeat of the Spanish Armada in 1588.

**Track chart of the Spanish Armada,** 1588, from *Expeditionis Hispaniorum in Angliam vera descriptio* by Robert Adams, published in London, 1588–90. An early example of English engraving.

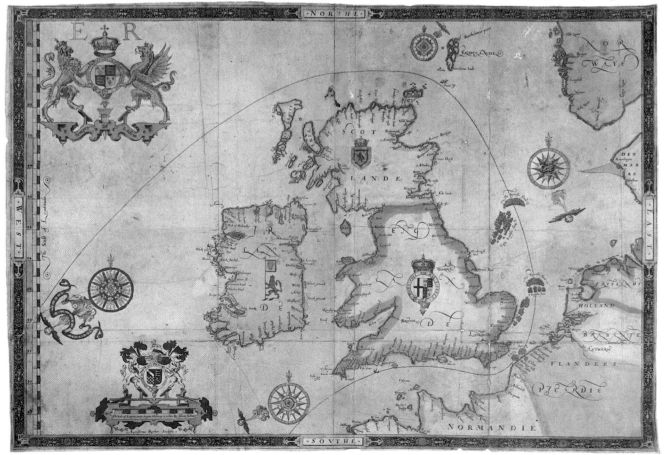

N° XVI.
*The Fifer's Credentials, addressed to his Captain.*

FOR THE SERVICE OF OUR COUNTRY

MARINE SOCIETY WAREHOUSE

**Young people** as illustrated in *Three letters on the subject of the Marine Society* by Jonas Hanway, published in London, 1758.

delightful illustrations, for the landsman was probably more able to see the eccentricities and humorous side of shipboard life than the seaman.

The invention and development of printing in the fifteenth century coincided with a critical moment in the history of European enterprise, when the educated, the skilled and the brave were planning and undertaking great voyages of discovery. These projects were extremely costly and required thorough preparation in training captains and officers in navigation, selecting seamen and assembling seaworthy ships and gear. The Portuguese, under the inspiration of Prince Henry the Navigator, first started to undertake long oceanic voyages after 1419, ultimately in search of the eastward trade route to India. The Spanish followed in the 1490s with their transatlantic enterprises, seeking a westward route to the same source of wealth.

One marked difference between the Spanish and

**A personal log** of a voyage from Bristol to the Mediterranean and back to London kept by the maritime artist Nicholas Pocock (1741–1821) aboard the *Betsey* in 1770. The India ink and wash drawings illustrate the weather, the ship and her sails.

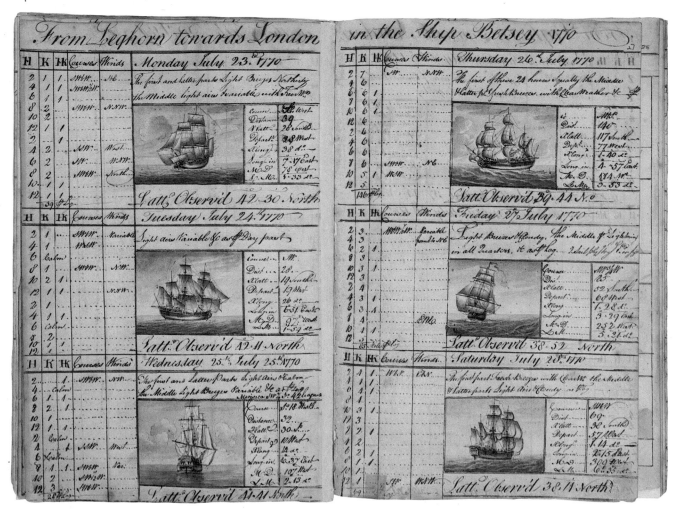

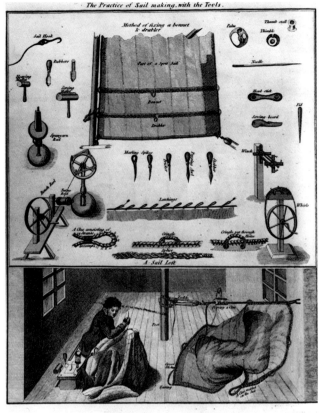

**An illustration of a 74-gun ship,** from *Liber Nauticus* by Dominick and John Thomas Serres, published in London, 1805. A fine example of a published illustration of the standard line of battleship of the late eighteenth and early nineteenth centuries.

**An illustration of sail making** from *The elements and practice of rigging and seamanship* by David Steel, published in London, 1794.

Portuguese approach to exploration was that the Spanish usually recorded the results of a voyage and made them available to those preparing for the next. Ten years after Christopher Columbus returned from his first great voyage, King Ferdinand and Queen Isabella established the Casa de Contratacion in Seville for the very purpose of codifying navigational and astronomical knowledge, to be used for training captains and for controlling trade. In this way the Spanish collected a large amount of valuable knowledge and later published it. This was embodied in the first great printed navigation manuals, such as that by Fernandez de Enciso, *Suma de Geografia* (Seville, 1519), and in what were perhaps the most influential navigation textbooks, *Arte de Navegar* (Valladolid, 1545) by Pedro de Medina and *Breve Compendio de la Sphera y de la Arte de Navegar* (Seville, 1551 and 1556) by Martin Cortes. These were later translated and published in Italian, French, Flemish, Dutch and English. Martin Cortes's work was translated into English by Richard Eden, and published in London in 1561. It became the chief source of navigational knowledge for English seamen and a most important factor in their rapid success as explorers and navigators.

Following the rediscovery, translation and publication of the work of the Greek geographer Ptolemy (the first edition without maps in Cologne in 1475, and the first edition with maps in Italy in 1477), a similar movement occurred in the production of maps and later of atlases. This answered and reflected the interest in voyages of discovery and their commercial and social importance. Notable examples are by Abraham Ortelius (1527–98), whose first atlas was published in Antwerp in 1570, Gerard Mercator (1512–94) and Willem Janszoon Blaeu (1571–1638). These various printing enterprises were among the first and most important manifestations of the spread of European maritime knowledge and expertise through publication.

From the early seventeenth century the Dutch and English took on the mantle of oceanic traders initiated by the Portuguese and the Spanish. However, it was the Dutch who took the lead, probably because more settled economic conditions allowed their merchant classes to develop trading enterprises more easily, and because these enterprises answered the need for an expanded national economy. Their interest in fine printing and the production of copper plate in neighbouring Germany gave them a further advantage, and it was the Dutch printing houses that published atlases until the 1670s. Seventeenth-century Amsterdam, as a wealthy commercial city supporting an active and zealous population of merchants and seamen, was ideal for the production of such works.

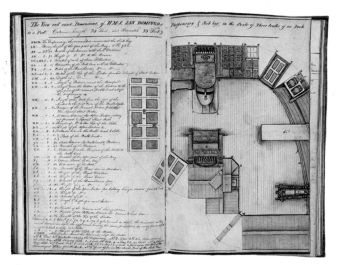

A manuscript diagram of a sick bay and dispensary aboard HM Ship *San Domingo c* 1812–14. From a watch and quarter bill belonging to Captain S. J. Pechell.

With the development of the European carrying trade in the sixteenth century and the establishment of a colonial empire in the East Indies in the seventeenth century, the need grew for printed manuals and 'rutters' (books which gave information on shipping routes). It was Waghenaer who published the first great 'waggoner' (an English term derived from his name) entitled *The Mariner's Mirror* in the English edition. This waggoner covered the European coastline and gave information on anchorages, tides, currents, instruments and tables. It also contained charts of coastlines and harbours, and silhouettes of landfalls. The first edition published in Dutch in 1584 was considered of such great importance that the Privy Council ordered an English translation. This was supervised by Anthony Ashley (1551–1627) and published in 1588 with a dedication to Sir Francis Drake. Other manuals were produced in different languages and in many editions.

**A first-rate ship at anchor** taken from *A new and universal dictionary of the marine ... enlarged by William Burney ...* by William Falconer, published in London, 1830.

The development of printed manuals on shipbuilding occurred much more slowly. Probably because of the jealous, protective power of the long-established shipwrights' guilds, records of their work are much rarer than those of the navigators, but with the enormously increased need for ships, the demand for books on shipbuilding grew. This was accelerated by the introduction of shipborne cannon, which initiated great changes in naval architecture and a whole new technique of sea warfare. In the hundred years between 1537 and 1637, enormous strides were made, and because of the oceanic activities of rival nations war became increasingly maritime in character. However, it was not until 1637 that the first book in English on shipbuilding appeared, Thomas Heywood's *A true description of HM Royal Ship*. This described King Charles's great new ship the *Sovereign of the Seas* and was published on the date of her launch. The earliest book in English on naval gunnery is William Bourne's translation of Tartaglia's *Art of Shooting in Great Ordinance*, published in 1587. The first book originating in English seems to be Thomas Smith's *The Art of Gunnerie* published in 1600, long after the first mounting of heavy cannon on board ship in the reign of Henry VIII.

As news of the great discoveries and of the possibilities of trade spread, interest widened and general demand for books on these subjects grew. At first, accounts of individual voyages and commentaries on them appeared, then projects for the expansion of trade. For the English, Spanish dominion of the western Atlantic and Portuguese dominion of the Indian Ocean gave rise to the need for accurate, reasonably priced and readily available books. Intellectuals such as Richard Eden (c 1521–76), Sir Humphrey Gilbert (c 1539–83) and Sir Walter Raleigh (c 1552–1618) were stimulated to write on exploration, trade, sea warfare and defence. In an attempt to circumvent seas dominated by the Spanish and Portuguese, the English were attracted to the possibility of a north-west passage round North America and of a north-east passage around Asia as routes to the trading riches of the East.

Later compilers such as Giovanni Battista Ramusio (1485–1557) and Richard Eden published editions of collective voyage accounts which sometimes include

**'Turning in'** and **'A lee lurch'** from *The Journal of a landsman from Portsmouth to Lisbon on board HMS ...* by Robert Seymour, published in London, 1831. ▷

HH Pinx.t        Printed by C. Motte Leic.r Sq.re        R. Seymour del.t

## TURNING IN.

HH Pinx.t        R. Seymour del.t

## A LEE LURCH.

London Published by Thos. McLean, 26 Haymarket 1831.

from Madge to get nothing rich which might possibly make us bilious, I very judiciously selected pork

◁ **Emigrants Departure!** Sketch taken from an illustrated diary kept by Alfred Withers aboard the clipper ship *James Baines* on a voyage from Liverpool to Melbourne in 1857.

**Salcombe,** an illustration from *A voyage round Great Britain in 1813* by Richard Ayton, with illustrative views by William Daniell (1769–1837), published in London, 1814–25.

little-known voyages. This work was continued by the celebrated Theodor De Bry (1528–98), Richard Hakluyt (1552–1616), Jan Huyghen Van Linschoten (1563–1611) and Samuel Purchas (1575–1626). These great books, with their finely engraved maps and illustrations, became standard works of reference and are still widely read. With the further development of publishing in the seventeenth and eighteenth centuries, it became common to publish accounts of voyages, and navigators such as William Dampier (1652–1715), Admiral Anson (1697–1762) and Captain James Cook (1728–79), all published accounts of their achievements.

◁ **Manuscript chart of Africa** by John B. Agnese, dated 1554. The Kingdom of Prester John is marked; the German title was added later.

The capital investment in both merchant and war ships, which by the late seventeenth century were operating on an almost world-wide basis, became substantial. Losses by shipwreck were common and extremely expensive, and it was appreciated that many of these were due to the lack of a proven reliable method of determining longitude. In Britain the Royal Observatory was founded at Greenwich in 1675 for the express purpose of solving the longitude problem and of improving standards of navigation at sea. The results of the work of the first Astronomer Royal, John Flamsteed, were first published (without his permission) by the Royal Society as the *Historiae Coelestis* in 1712. Flamsteed was dissatisfied with the standard of this work, and as soon as opportunity allowed he obtained three hundred of the four hundred copies and burnt them as 'a sacrifice to Heavenly Truth', salvaging those pages of which he did approve for later publication. He (and later his widow) subsequently destroyed as many as possible of the remaining hundred copies.

**Acquittance from Prince Henry the Navigator to his Chancellor, Goncalo de Sousa,** signed by Prince Henry and dated 11 January 1458.

The Museum has the unique copy owned by the second Astronomer Royal, Edmond Halley, much annotated by him and probably at proof stage in publication. The final approved edition was completed by Joseph Crosthwaite and published in 1725 after Flamsteed's death.

The spread of interest in travel created a demand for pictures of the places, people and customs observed by voyagers. It was much in the interests of publishers of both travel books and of manuals to satisfy these demands and, thanks to the development of line engraving on copper, illustrated books abounded in the seventeenth, eighteenth and nineteenth centuries. The invention of etching, mezzotinting and, later, aquatinting gave the printer a wide choice of method. Each was best suited to a particular subject, for example, stipple engraving and mezzotinting to portraiture. In the nineteenth century many beautifully illustrated topographical books were published, such as *A Voyage Round Great Britain* by William Daniel (London, 1814–25). In addition, books on seamanship such as *The Young Sea Officers Sheet Anchor* by Darcy Lever (London, 1808), David Steel's *The Elements and Practice of Rigging and Seamanship* (London, 1794), John Charnocks' *Marine Architecture* (London, 1880–02), were all very finely illustrated with engravings of parts of ships, rigging, equipment and views of ship manoeuvres.

In the early years the regular publication of Almanacs for general use was followed by the publication of periodicals, such as those by the scientific societies. The *Philosophical Transactions of the Royal Society*, first published in 1666, were the earliest. These not only kept the reader informed of scientific developments, but were reasonably priced to members and later to general subscribers. Books became a fundamental statutory reference and teaching tool and over the years more and more available to the ordinary man and less the prerogative of the wealthy and highly educated. The printed manual is an essential item on the shipborne shelves of the seaman: even with radar and other sophisticated devices, no navigator would get underway without his appropriate pilot books and manuals.

The formation of the collection of printed books and manuscripts at the National Maritime Museum owes much to the Museum's great benefactor, Sir James Caird. Through Sir James, many very valuable books

**Two amusing drawings of ship board life from a private log** kept by John L. Kirby, Second Officer aboard the Blackwall sailing ship *Owen Glendower* on a voyage from London to Bombay and back in 1846/7. They show the bosun with his call and the carpenter caulking the deck.

and manuscripts were acquired in the 1930s, at a time when fewer private collectors and institutions were buying. Thanks also to the generosity and scholarship of such figures as Dr. R. C. Anderson (1883–1976), formerly Chairman of Trustees, the Museum is also rich in early books on shipbuilding, signalling and seamanship. The Library also has examples of many of the early books on navigation, of a very early rutter book by Pierre Garcie, published in 1542, and a beautiful edition of *The Mariner's Mirror* of 1588. Similarly, early British books on astronomy, seamanship, gunnery and navigation are well represented and the shelves are very richly endowed with accounts of voyages, particularly the collective works of Ramusio, Purchas, Hakluyt and De Bry. With the considerable additions made in recent years, the Museum can reasonably claim to possess one of the finest specialist libraries on maritime history and related subjects in existence.

The collections of manuscripts are considerable. They are particularly rich in personal papers but cover all aspects of British seafaring from the fourteenth to the twentieth century. They include the great *Waggoner of the Pacific coast of the Americas* by William Hack

(fl. 1680–1710) made in 1685, and Public Records of naval administration and ships, particularly relating to the Navy Board, the Admiralty, and dockyard administration in the eighteenth and nineteenth centuries. There are such famous items as the journal kept by Edward Barlow (b. 1642) during his many voyages, letters from Lord Nelson, the papers of Sir Charles Middleton (later Lord Barham) and documents relating to the lives and achievements of almost all the nation's famous seamen, as well as many not so well known but whose lives throw light on our national history.

The Museum now has a fine collection of material covering the activities of merchant shipping services, such as Lloyds Register, and of companies such as P&O, Shaw Savill, Royal Mail, British India and Furness Withy. Of particular interest is the collection of the Henley family, which is a very complete record of their shipping operations between the years 1770 and 1813. There are also the records of the Shipbuilders and Repairers National Association, and of shipbuilding yards such as William Denny and Brothers, John L. Thornycroft and Co., Green and Silley Weir, and of the specialist yacht builders Camper & Nicholsons. Samples

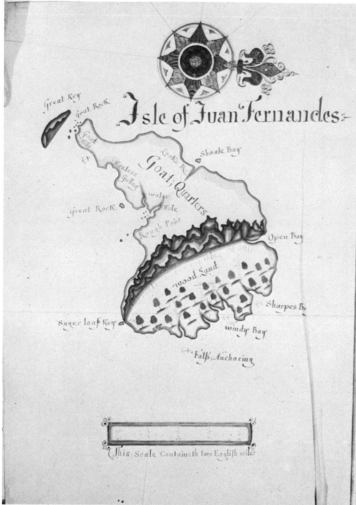

**The island of Juan Fernandes** off the West coast of South America. Alexander Selkirk was marooned on this island, and his story inspired Defoe to write Robinson Crusoe. From the Waggoner made by William Hack, 1685.

of the records of the Registrar General of Shipping and Seamen are also held by the Museum. The manuscript collections are all listed in the two volume *Guide to the Manuscripts at the National Maritime Museum.*

Thus the maritime historian or interested layman has a wealth of documentary and printed evidence of the past methods, achievements, habits and failures of British seamen, shipbuilders, owners and managers available to him. Of course many early records were destroyed long before the Museum was founded, and in the case of recent business records, much thinning of material took place on the grounds of space before the

era of cheap microfilm and photographic reproduction rendered this unnecessary.

The historian needs the printed and manuscript records as his basic evidence; they are vital to the understanding of our national history and character, and in the words of Dr. Johnson, 'Knowledge is of two kinds. We know a subject ourselves, or we know where we can find information upon it. When we enquire into any subject, the first thing we have to do is to know what books have treated of it. This leads us to look at catalogues and at the backs of books in libraries.'

# Weapons and Antiquities

JOHN MUNDAY

*Head of the Department of Weapons & Antiquities*

'Weapons' is perhaps not the best label for a collection which might rather be called 'Martial and Maritime', for while the underlying themes are those of attack and defence and their implications, much beauty and high craftsmanship is also in evidence. Mars is in the ascendant while Neptune provides the setting. The rich variety of fine objects in the Greenwich collections which are classified as 'Antiquities' are all, in a sense, commemorative. Many of them are souvenirs of success, but there are also reminders of death, and souvenirs of survival for both men and ships – relics which have been carefully preserved and inscribed. Among other intriguing exhibits are old-fashioned ship fittings, tools, implements and sailors' possessions. Not only some of the contents of ships and their cabins are collected, but also the contents of sea chests and even of seamen's pockets.

## Guns

The Museum does not possess a fully comprehensive collection of guns of all types and periods, but with scale models as well as real pieces of naval artillery, either on show or in reserve, a representative range is being built up. The surviving examples of ships' main armament in bronze or iron show little change in three centuries – the general appearance of the smooth bore muzzle loader did not alter very much on land or sea. The wrought iron gun recovered in 1836 from the wreck of Henry VIII's warship the *Mary Rose* of 1545, the earliest gun in the Museum, is however very different: it fired stone shot and was loaded by means of a detachable breech chamber. Underwater archaeologists are currently bringing up more guns from the same wreck off Portsmouth, and it is interesting to find in the ship cast bronze guns

△ **Tudor Gun from *Mary Rose*** lost in 1545. The massive eroded timber bed of an iron bombard is seen from the rear, with grooves which held the banded gun barrel, and beside it the remains of the chamber with a stone shot in place.

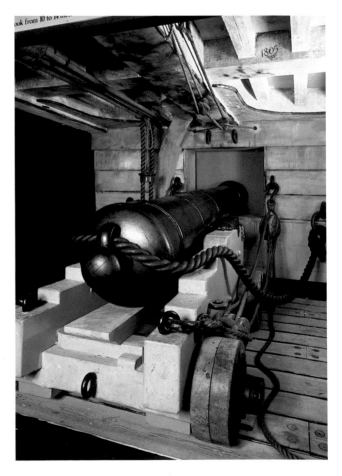

**Great Gun of the Nelson period.** The twenty-four pounder muzzle loader on a truck carriage with heavy breeching rope and tackles had a crew of 10–14 men. Overhead were kept the rammer, sponge and worm.

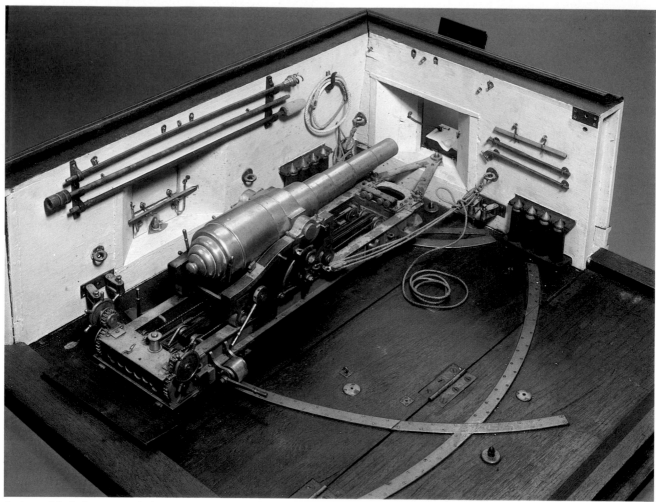

**Scale model of 38-ton gun of 1874** on a double pivot slide for firing on broadside or bow. This weapon of the ironclad era was still a muzzle loader, but it was rifled and fired cylinderical projectiles with conical heads. Sponge, rammer and worm are still in evidence.

of the type which lasted into Queen Victoria's reign. These were the conventional ship weapons, cannon and culverines, known as the Great Guns. Almost the only variant was the carronade, from the Carron foundry in Scotland. It was shorter, lighter, fired a big shot for its size and was deadly at close range. There was a notable improvement in firing mechanisms in the introduction of flintlocks for the Great Guns, instead of the uncertain 'slow match', by Captain Sir Charles Douglas in 1782.

Iron ships which replaced the 'wooden walls' in the nineteenth century needed larger and more powerful guns in battle. The technology of shot and shell, of rifled barrel and improved powder supplied the means, and

**Firearms:** sea service percussion pistol with belt-clip and butt-ring for lanyard (*top right*); pair of silver mounted officer's flint-lock pistols with powder flask and bullet mould (*left*); pair of flink-lock brass mounted pistols with hinged ramrods, the trigger guards engraved *Pleiad* (the African exploring ship of 1854) (*right*); revolver by Adams, *c* 1851, with tools (*below*).

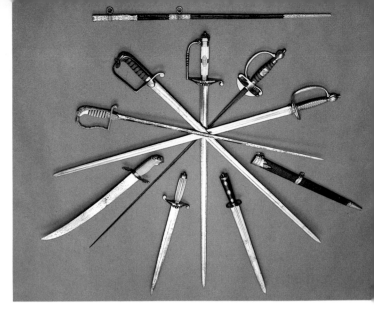

**Swords and Dirks** (*clockwise from vertical*): spadroon with '5-ball' beaded hilt, 1795; small-sword for masters, pursers and medical officers, 1825; oval side-ring pattern hilt *c* 1785; dirk and scabbard of Sir William Cornwallis; dirk with '5-ball' beaded hilt; curved dirk of volunteer or midshipman, 1800; decorated dress sword of Admiral, 1810, with scabbard; straight stirrup hilt with black grip, the 1825 pattern for Masters and Warrant Officers.

famous names from British industrial history marked the development of the naval gun as we know it. Sir William Armstrong reintroduced the breechloading system (an echo back to the *Mary Rose*) while the precision engineers Whitworth, Vickers and many others made their contributions to the involved evolution of twentieth-century gunnery.

The collection of firearms ranges from sea-service flintlock pistols, brass-mounted with belt clips for easy carriage, to muskets and rifles, and includes some presentation pieces of superb quality which were carried by officers of distinction. Percussion caps later succeeded flint and steel, and the rifled barrel replaced the smooth bore. These weapons gave two expressions to the English language – 'a flash in the pan', which happened when a piece missed fire, and 'blowing great guns' which recalls the thunder of artillery and refers to the roar of gale force winds. Sailors were trained for landing parties and fought on shore alongside the Royal Marines and the army in many campaigns across the globe, to which their medals and battle honours bear witness.

## Swords

The hanger and the cutlass were probably the first swords for seamen. A shorter weapon was best for hacking and thrusting one's way through the close fighting which took place on a ship's deck. The fighting swords and dress swords eventually became two distinct categories: the first eminently serviceable, without decoration, stout and somewhat heavy; whilst for ceremonial occasions a lighter weapon was worn – elegant, ornamental, but equally deadly in skilled hands. A third type of sword was the presentation weapon, capable of being worn but so ornamental that serious use would ruin its good looks and its high value.

The Navy did not regulate the pattern of officers' swords until 1805, the years of the Battle of Trafalgar. The stirrup hilt, with an ivory grip and a straight tapered blade, which could vary in length according to choice, gave a balanced thrusting sword of a type which was already popular. The spadroon, with a distinctive beaded hilt, was much used by infantry and naval officers, and the curved light-infantry weapon is also found ornamented with naval emblems and nautical decorations.

The small-sword, weapon of the gentleman and

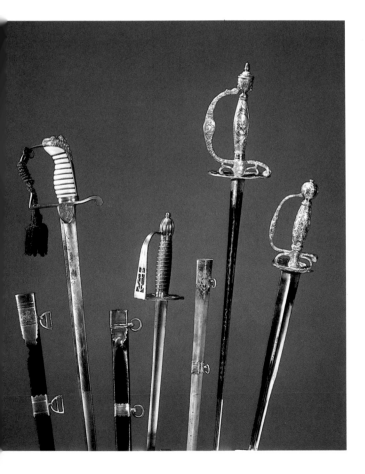

**Swords of the Admirals** (*from left*): 1805 pattern, Lord St. Vincent; slotted hilt with anchor, Lord Collingwood; small-sword with silver-gilt hilt, Sir William Cornwallis; French silver-gilt small-sword with *colichemarde* blade, Earl Howe, KG.

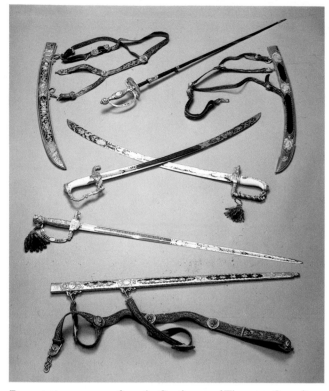

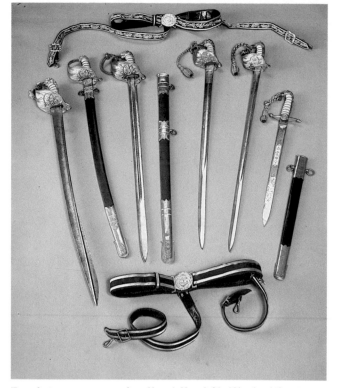

**Presentation weapons:** from the Gentlemen of Thanet to Capt. Sir Thomas Staines, 1809, value 200 guineas, with scabbard and belt (*below*); from the merchants of Trinidad to Capt. Columbine, 1804, value 500 guineas, with scabbard and belt at left (*above left*); Lloyd's Patriotic Fund to Capt. Wilson of the East Indiaman *Warley*, 1804, with scabbard and belt at right (*right*); from the City of London to Sir John Jervis, silver-gilt small-sword set with enamel plaques and diamonds, value 200 guineas, 1797 (*top*).

**Regulation patterns, to date** (*from left*): solid half-basket hilt, pipe-back blade, 1827; flag officer's scabbard with oak-leaf decoration, one locket with two rings, 1847–56; commissioned officer's sword with claymore blade, and scabbard, 1872; Wilkinson blade 1891; Royal Naval Air Service badge on hilt, 1914; Midshipman's dirk with scabbard, 1901; full dress belt for flag officers, 1901 (*above*); full dress belt for Lieutenants, 1901 (*below*).

descendant of the rapier of earlier days, was universally worn as a dress sword throughout the eighteenth century; indeed senior officers probably wore this type only. The hilt, often silver or silver-gilt, sometimes bore designs appropriate to the wearer's pursuits: for the naval officer a trophy of guns, anchors and flags, sails and rudders, or a Neptune with dolphins, shells and sea weed, would be appropriate.

In 1827 a brass half-basket hilt embossed with a crowned anchor was introduced and the style is still in use today. The pipe-backed blade on which it was originally mounted was unsatisfactory, however, and the broad-grooved blade introduced in 1847 found a wider appeal. The dirk or short sword of the midshipman was a useful weapon in small boats and was sometimes worn by senior officers. A dirk could match a sword in style and decoration but was evidently not worn at the same time, unlike the earlier dagger. From 1825 midshipmen were ordered to wear swords of a length proportionate to their stature, so a small officer would have worn one of the small light swords also encountered. The dirk reappeared in 1856 and lasted as long as the midshipman's dress was the waist-length 'round-jacket'. Seamen wore short curved swords, often without any nautical

symbol to distinguish them from military weapons. The earlier pattern cutlass had a distinctive hilt, the guard being fashioned from sheet steel in the two-disc design common to various navies.

In 1803 the Corporation of Lloyds established their Patriotic Fund which, among other awards, gave presentation swords of three different values in recognition of distinguished action against the country's enemies: the defence of sea-borne trade was recognized as protection of the nation's life-blood, and the defeat of a hostile fleet removed a threat to mercantile prosperity no less than it affected the political scene. Richly ornamental swords were awarded by governments, such as the Assembly of Jamaica to naval commanders who had warded off the depredations of enemies intent on destroying the great and vulnerable merchant fleets on which our economy depended. The proud City of London gave superb jewelled and enamelled small-swords, beautifully decorated with symbolic and heraldic allusions to the victor and his victory. The West India Merchants, too, were a power in the Common Council of the City and their gratitude for outstanding services such as the protection of valuable convoys was often marked by presentation weapons.

## Costume

The Museum's collection of costume consists mainly of naval uniform, the largest part of which belonged to officers whose expensive formal dress was often carefully stored away, rather than to seamen, whose dress was much more simple, subject to great wear and tear and has unfortunately not often survived. Where there are gaps in our knowledge of dress worn at sea, one can turn to the Museum's picture collection for evidence.

In the reign of George II, naval officers petitioned for a uniform so that they would be recognized as belonging to the King's service. Previously they had worn what their taste and pocket dictated. Their petition was successful and in 1748 approved specimens of the full-skirted blue coats with white facings and gilt buttons, called the 'sealed patterns', were made. Several examples of these have survived at Greenwich. In the centuries that followed, clothing became simpler and the undress uniform of one period became the full dress of the succeeding one. Although the cut of the garments usually followed civilian fashion, distinctive features persisted, such as the slashed mariner's cuff.

Familiar names for sailors, such as Jack Tar and Bluejacket, referred to their waterproof tarpaulin garments and to the distinctive short coats they wore. For the Navy before 1857, clothing contractors provided bulk supplies so that there was a certain uniformity in dress and the seaman was instantly recognizable. This clothing was known generally as 'slops' from the slop-hose or loose over-trousers which were once the occupational dress of seamen and fishermen. In all seaports slopsellers carried stocks of new and second-hand clothing. The first uniform regulations for sailors in the Navy date from 1857 when the blue jean collar with its three rows of white tape and the black silk neckerchief (which are sometimes mistakenly associated with Nelson's victories and death) were officially ordered to be worn. In fact this simply regularized what had been the most favoured dress to have evolved from the seamen's clothes of the previous century.

For officers, informal and thus undignified dress in one age became the accepted thing in the next. Peaked caps, introduced for wear on board ship only, were a practical alternative to the high cocked hat and eventually received approval. Trousers such as the seamen wore finally ousted the knee breeches and stockings of the officers and the short jacket without tails was in time allowed for everyday wear. Gold bands, rings, stripes or rows of woven wire lace were a convenient way of indicating rank, and in fact this eighteenth-century idea

**The first uniform,** the surviving 'sealed' patterns of 1748: single-breasted dress coat and waistcoat of a Lieutenant (*left*); his Frock or undress coat which could be worn single or double-breasted (*right*).

**The 1774 Regulations:** Captain's full dress coat and waistcoat with plain anchor buttons (*left*); Captain over three years seniority, undress coat with buttons grouped in threes denoting rank (*right*). Both could be worn double-breasted.

**Regulation patterns of 1795 and 1812:** Admiral's full dress worn until 1812, which belonged to Sir William Cornwallis (d. 1819) (*left*); Captain's full dress worn until 1830, with white facings and crown and anchor buttons (*right*). Both could be worn double-breasted.

**Admirals of the Fleet:** Full dress worn by HRH the Duke of Windsor KG as King Edward VIII, 1936 (*left*); Frock coat of Lord Fisher of Kilverstone, 1905 (*right*).

**Seamen**. White suit made on board HM Yacht for the Prince of Wales 1846 (*right*). The first regulation seaman's uniform of 1857 was very like the Prince's suit: white duck frock with small sleeve badge of 1st Class Petty Officer, 1855 (*left*); blue jacket with gold wire device of 1st Class Petty Officer with three good conduct badges, 1879 (*centre*); straw sennit hat, worn until 1921 (*below*).

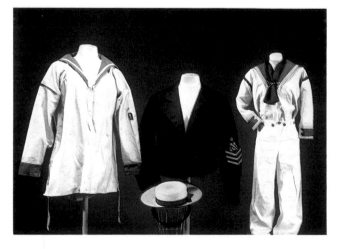

is still in use today both in the Royal and the Merchant Navy.

It was a seaman's garment that introduced the words 'grog' and 'groggy' into the English language. Admiral Vernon's habit of wearing a grogram (grosgrain) cloak earned him the nickname 'Old Grog'; the daily ration of watered-down rum he introduced for his men became 'grog', and the feeling of over indulgence therein, 'groggy'.

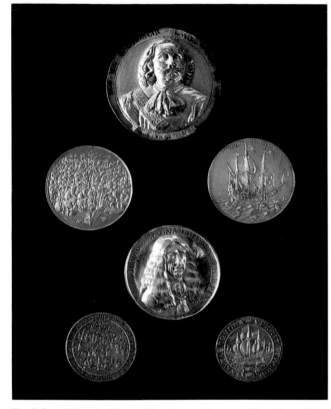

**English and Dutch ships and battles on silver medals:** defeat of the Spanish Armada, 1588 (*lower left*); embarkation of Charles II from Scheveningen for his Restoration, 1660 (*centre*); Kortenaar, Lieutenant-Admiral of Holland, killed in the Battle of Lowestoft, 1665 (*top*).

**Gold awards:** Admiral Sir William Penn, father of the founder of Pennsylvania, received this massive gold chain and medal from the Commonwealth after the First Dutch War, 1653 (*left*); naval reward of James II, 1685 (*within, top*); Commonwealth medal to Captains (*within below*); King's gold medal and chain to flag officers, to Alexander Hood, Lord Bridport for the 1st June 1794 (*right*); George III, commemorating British victories 1798 (*within top*); King's gold medal for Captains, instituted 1796 (*within below*).

## The Medal Room

The gleam and glitter of medals and decorations offset by the lustre of silk ribbons in many colours encourages the visitor to closer examination. All the exhibits here are linked by a maritime theme: a struggle between men at sea and between men and the sea. Representations of monarchs and their sea commanders, their ships and their battles, dating from the fourteenth century to the present time, appear by virtue of the medallist's art. Recurring decorative features are dolphins, anchors, sails, tridents, cannon, zephyrs, rocks and waves, seen of course against the changing shape of ships.

The works of the greatest medallists, Dutch, French, German, Italian and our own British artists are found here in unrivalled profusion. Not all medals were designed to be worn, and medallions to commemorate launches, anniversaries, inventions and discoveries are shown beside the campaign medals and their clasps or bars indicating battle honours gained all over the world.

**Private medals:** Matthew Boulton, Engineer, presented this to all Trafalgar survivors (*above*); Admiral Lord St Vincent issued his own medal to those who served under him in 1800 (*below*).

**Groups in the Medal Room.** (*From top left*) Victoria Cross to Able Seaman Robinson, Naval Brigade, Indian Mutiny 1857; Victoria Cross, Distinguished Service Order, Reserve Decoration and U.S. Navy Cross, etc, to Lieutenant Ronald Niel Stuart RNR, later Commodore Canadian Pacific Line. (*From centre left*). Officer of the Order of the British Empire; Distinguished Service Cross and medals of both World Wars; Distinguished Service Medal, World War I and Long Service Medal to Chief Petty Officer. (*Below centre*) D.S.M., Merchant Navy Medal World War I. (*Below left*) Naval General Service Medal, 1848, with six clasps. (*Centre*) Queen Victoria Arctic Medal and other campaign medals including clasps.

Crosses and stars in recognition of bravery and distinguished service and orders of chivalry, some belonging to long extinct royal houses, are grouped under the names of famous men who won them. Nearby are awards made to simple seamen for valour in action, long service or devotion to duty. The serene profiles of heads of State, classically laurelled, contrast with the likenesses of admirals and captains who were the victors and occasionally the victims, engaged in their country's struggle for supremacy on the seas.

The role of the common sailor was not forgotten, and early in Victoria's reign the Naval General Service Medal was issued to those still living in 1848 who had fought in the wars of George III, dating back to 1793. This, in silver, carried clasps on its ribbon for each of a man's naval actions and was awarded to ordinary seamen and admirals alike.

Coins form part of the collection, too, from the gold noble of Edward III showing his ship of 1340, a symbol of emerging sea power, to the bronze trade tokens of the Napoleonic war when the ship design was an indication of Britain's dependence both on seaborne trade and its protecting Navy.

**A distinguished career:** Admiral Sir Frederick G. D. Bedford's Grand Cross of the Order of St Michael and St George, with Collar, Star and sash; campaign medals of forty years active service, with miniatures beneath (*below*); Orders of St John and the Turkish Medjidie (*left*); his Grand Cross of the Order of the Bath (*right*).

**Trophies.** A silver dish engraved with Piet Heyn's capture of a Spanish plate fleet in Cuba, 1628, is also inscribed as a Christening present; the silver-gilt lidded tankard is set with Spanish coins from a rich capture by HMS *Naiad* in 1799.

**Presentation plate.** Punchbowl engraved with portrait of the snow *Earl of Bute* and dedication to her Master, 1767; tankard given by the Admiralty to Master Shipwright John Holland for launching HMS *Captain*, 1743; and candlesticks from the same to John Phillips for launching HMS *Feversham*, 1712.

## Plate

The presentation of a piece of plate – it might be an urn, candlesticks, a punchbowl, a tea or coffee service, a tray or a tankard – was a way of rewarding merit which might range from the successful launching of a ship or the defence of a valuable merchantman, to victory in battle or the saving of life at sea. The many fine pieces at Greenwich were collected, not as examples of the art of the silversmith, but as testimonials to heroism, fortitude, devotion to duty and many other virtues.

One fine early example is the Dutch dish made from captured Spanish silver, engraved with Admiral Piet Heyn's portrait and a view of his resounding action of 1628. In the eighteenth century Lord Duncan received several handsome pieces, one in 1782 from an admirer and others after the battle of Camperdown in 1797, from various Scottish municipalities. Nelson had an inscribed dinner service from Lloyds in two instalments in recognition of the Nile and Copenhagen. The gift of a snuff box in precious metal was another way of marking approbation and esteem. The redoubtable Admiral Edward Vernon was given the Freedom of the City of London in 1740 and the scroll was contained in a fine gold box. The Museum possesses presentation boxes for other admirals honoured in the same way: Sir Robert Stopford, who commanded the fleet which bombarded the fortress of Acre in the campaign of 1840, was given his Freedom in a casket modelled in the shape of the

**The Lighthouse Fort,** strongpoint of Algiers' defences, bombarded by Lord Exmouth's fleet, 1816, is flanked by groups of British sailors freeing Christian slaves and overcoming Algerine captors. Paul Storr's silver-gilt table centrepiece was given to the Admiral by his officers: value 1400 guineas.

**Cups or vases** (*from left*): the Hon. East India Company to Captain John Allen of the *Duke of Dorset*, 1759; lion-topped, the Lloyd's Patriotic Fund Vase is one of 66 presented between 1804 and 1809 for gallant actions; Admiral Sir Francis Geary's silver cup commemorated services as a Captain at Louisbourg, 1745.

fort; Lord Rodney's simple oval gold box was given him by Cork in 1782; while Nelson's freedom box from Thetford in his native Norfolk is an oak piece mounted in silver. Another golden fortress tops the centrepiece given to Lord Exmouth after the bombardment of Algiers in 1816 when many Christian slaves were set free. Later on, caskets suitable for cigars or cigarettes became more usual; Queen Alexandra gave her sailor son George V a silver box by Fabergé, ornamented with famous warships in relief.

Silver vinaigrettes decorated with ship designs and sold as souvenirs after Trafalgar are among the smaller silver exhibits, and other battle commemoratives include a pocket cigarette case with an enamelled picture recalling Jutland in 1916. Personal gifts, watches, rings and other items of jewellery decorated with nautical symbols or inscriptions of maritime interest, are also included in the collection. The seamen had their tobacco and snuff boxes, too; one in copper is roughly engraved with the scene of the loss by accident of HMS *Royal George* in 1782, and a similar box in copper and brass is inscribed with the name of its owner and his ship, HMS *Perseus*, which fought in the War of American Independence.

**Gold boxes from the City of London** with its Freedom to Admiral Edward Vernon, 1740 (*top*). To Lord Bridport for his action off L'Orient, 1795 (*centre left*); To Captain Sir Edward Berry for the Nile, 1798, with enamel view of the battle (*centre right*); and the engraved base showing his command (and Nelson's flagship) HMS *Vanguard* (*below right*); to Sir John Jervis for successes in the West Indies, 1793, with his arms in enamel (*below left*).

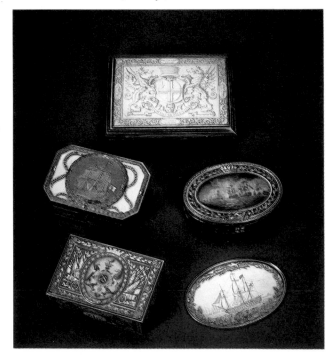

**Commemorative pottery on naval themes** began with Admiral Edward Vernon's capture of Porto Bello in 1739. He stands victorious on the salt-glaze tea-pot, and his ships bombard the Spanish fortress on the delftware plates. The tankard (*left*) dated 1741 may depict his attack on Cartagena.

## Ceramics

It is remarkable that the idea of producing pottery to celebrate a naval victory does not seem to have occurred until 1739, after Vernon's capture of Porto Bello, for from that date onwards jugs, mugs, bowls, cups and pots depicting naval leaders and their triumphs in each successive war were produced in large numbers. Admiral Rodney appears in various forms, inscribed with toasts such as 'Success to Brave Rodney'. His greatest battle, the Saints in 1782, is also commemorated for his Captain, Sir Charles Douglas, in a Chinese export punchbowl decorated with a copy of an engraved battlepiece and his coat of arms. Keppel, Howe, Duncan and Nelson all appear on pottery while their sailors, who were always popular, are represented in 'Toby' jugs and earthenware figures. Groups on the theme of the sailor's farewell are usually paired with those showing his happy return. Portrait figures include Captain Cook, Albert Edward, Prince of Wales in his sailor suit, as well as Admirals Napier and Dundas at the time of the Russian War in 1855.

Notable among foreign porcelain is the Copenhagen punchbowl, one of a limited edition made in honour of the Danish defenders of their capital against the British attack in 1801. An English Minton bowl is the twentieth-century counterpart, made to commemorate the surrender of the German fleet to the Grand Fleet in 1918.

Seaborne trade, the fisheries, merchant ships and their crews, captains and owners are commemorated on lively Liverpool wares of the eighteenth century and by the pink lustred Sunderland pottery of the following century, with its transfer scenes and doggerel verses. This was mostly tavern or cottage ware and is lucky to have survived. Some of it was probably used at sea, but mess and saloon china marked with ship or company names did not appear until the first half of the nineteenth century. Grand domestic services are represented in the Museum by Nelson's personal china bearing his crests and coat of arms and by monogrammed pieces from the Royal Yachts.

The collection also has engraved glasses, fashionable for toasting a launch or a successful sea-trading venture and showing merchant vessels with perhaps the owner's or master's initials on them. Naval victories were also commemorated by this engraved glassware, and Nelson's funeral procession with his ship-like hearse was also popular. Privateers – ships licensed to raid the enemy's commerce in reprisal – seem often to have had glasses engraved for them, for theirs was a risky business and all concerned would wish them good fortune.

**Health to Lord Rodney** expressed in different ways. In 1782 there was a large output of ware in honour of his victory of The Saints, which gave the country a welcome success in the War that lost the American colonies.

**Nelson commemorative jugs and mugs** in cheerful pottery surround a porcelain cup and saucer from his own breakfast set, decorated with his coat of arms and crests. A hurried potter used an unmistakable portrait of Rodney to go with his 'Success to Adml Nelson' (*top left*).

**Punch bowls**, very necessary for convivial drinking. The Battle of The Saints, 1782, is commemorated in Chinese porcelain decorated with a copy of an English print (*left*); a Liverpool delftware bowl with portrait of a small merchantman of the *Hadwen* (*centre*); and a Copenhagen porcelain bowl showing Danish resistance to Nelson's bombardment in 1801 (*right*).

**The Lass that Loves a Sailor.** The Ralph Wood pair (*left*) and the blue and white version of the sailor, show typical seaman's dress of about 1780. The 'Departure' and 'Return', Staffordshire groups, are Nelson period, but where are the lasses to go with the sailors on the right?

▷

**Sailmaker's shop.** Whether afloat or on shore the sailmaker was surrounded by canvas, rope, needles, threads and his leather *palm*, and was seated at his bench with a sail tensioned across his knees. This figure uses the tools of an actual north Devon sailmaker, Braund of Braunton.

**Boatbuilder's shed,** ideally suited for wood on the damp river margins. The augers, adzes, mauls and other scattered equipment surround a boat with damaged stem-piece which is in for repair. A new one is being built alongside.

## Tools

The tools of the shipwright, sailmaker, cooper, armourer, carpenter and other craftsmen are also symbols of the age of sail. The skill of the seaman in ropework, which was usually both ornamental and of practical use, illustrates an age when hands and eyes were not often idle. Without possessing the glamour of weapons, the beauty of the caulking mallet, the adze, the sailmaker's palm, the fid and the serving mallet lies in their worn appearance, evidence of purposeful handling and long use. Some tools, like the sailmaker's seam rubber, made perhaps from whale ivory or from hardwood, are decorated. The ship's carpenter and his mates were key men, ensuring the hull, masts and spars were kept in good repair, and the cooper was always busy meeting demands for the storage of wet and dry goods like wine, salt meat, lentils and gunpowder – everything from stores to cargo.

The seaman's jack-knife, without which he was not considered properly dressed, was an essential tool. It usually carried a small marline spike for making splices and knots in rope, and the decorative possibilities of such everyday work were well understood by seamen. Bell-ropes, sea-chest handles, mats and numerous embellishments to the ship's fittings were often a source of great pride to captain and crew.

The seaman would also use his knife to fashion objects like model ships, while many a ship's carpenter deftly turned his hand to a bit of cabinet work or inlay in

**Seaman's crafts.** A ship portrait is depicted inside the lid of a seaman's chest, which has strong ornamental rope handles; another lies at the front. Ornate bell-ropes, a macramé 3-tier 'pocket' and two woolwork pictures of warships, *c* 1860, illustrate other seamen's crafts. Souvenirs like the mounted albatross beak, the shark's vertebrae and whale-ivory walking sticks, the ship in a bottle and the *scrimshaw* sperm whale tooth, are usual.

his spare time. Whether from boredom or simply from the urge to be creative, men off-watch usually turned to finer work. Woolwork pictures, popular at home from about the mid-nineteenth century, were a convenient handicraft which was easily stowed away: portraits of battleships, frigates, trading brigs and clippers, properly rigged and with proud bunting flying, appear off headlands capped with lighthouses or flagstaffs. On whaling ships *scrimshaw* work was a speciality of the sailors – whales' teeth were engraved with scenes of the fishery or copies of engravings, and useful articles were also fashioned from the ivory.

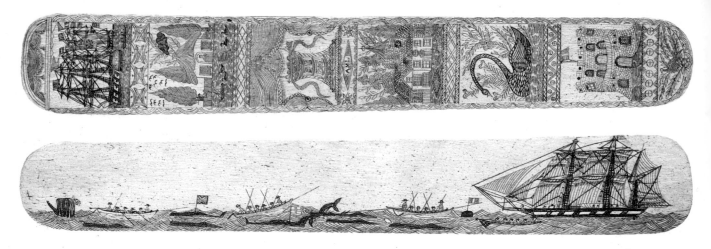

**Keepsake.** This whalebone stay busk or stiffener was worked by a whaleman in decorative panels with cottage and church, indicating thoughts of home. The other side bears a whaling scene.

## Furniture and Fittings

The seagoing furniture and ship fittings in the Museum range from the sailor's sea-box to the admiral's dressing chest, from a brass lamp to a large ship's steering wheel in teak. Some saloon furniture from the great ocean liners would not look out of place in a town house, and the floating palaces of the early twentieth century are indeed represented by exhibits from a royal residence – HM Yacht *Victoria & Albert III*. Also in the collection are examples of the folding washstands found in the cabins of passenger ships, while at the other extreme plain, timeless leather chairs and a couch which furnished Nelson's cabin in the *Victory* are to be seen. Lifting handles, rings and brass eye-bolts for securing furniture at sea are features of maritime pieces, which had to be lashable and stowable. Again, combination furniture similar to military 'campaign' secretaire chests supplied comfort and utility on long voyages under sail. Seamen often decorated their sea chests with a portrait of their ship inside the lid.

Carved work such as trophies, figures, perhaps the royal arms, could be found inboard as well as on the ship's hull, and examples can be seen in the collection alongside massive circular brass tompions – stoppers for ships' guns – and cast brass boat badges, all bearing heraldic designs. There are also several fine ships' bells, ranging from that of the Spanish *San Josef* of 1797 to that of the liner *Mauretania* of 1907. Port and starboard lights, shuttered signal lanterns and hanging, weighted

candle holders gimballed to remain upright, as well as shaded saloon lights which once swung to the motion of the ship, are all part of an unglamorous but nevertheless evocative display. There is even a saloon table designed to stay horizontal by swinging on an arc, from the royal racing cutter *Britannia*.

**Officer's chest,** about 1800, convenient for small cabins. This mahogany compactum contained writing and toilet materials as well as a wash-bowl and writing or reading slope. The brass carrying handles allowed it to be lashed in position at sea.

## Relics

Greenwich became a place of pilgrimage when the body of Nelson was brought to lie in state in the Painted Hall of the Royal Hospital in January 1806. The funeral was one of the greatest spectacles London had ever seen and souvenirs of the occasion, as well as commemorative pieces in mourning for the fallen hero, were produced all over the country. The ship-like funeral car, which was afterwards exhibited in the Painted Hall, is represented by the graceful figurehead, the only part remaining. Nelson's undress coat with the bullet hole in the shoulder was presented to the Hospital in 1845, and other relics of the great man were added over the years. The stories of Nelson's exploits and the manner of his death have endured to a remarkable degree as inspiration to succeeding generations.

Another outstanding figure of an earlier time, the circumnavigator Captain James Cook, has a gallery devoted to his achievements. His portrait and personal possessions, furniture and native artifacts brought back from his three momentous voyages of discovery, have been gazed upon by millions of visitors from all over the world. His death was the tragic climax to years of quite extraordinary endeavour in both nautical and scientific spheres, and its bicentenary was celebrated in 1979. The celebrations included researches into Cook's life and death.

**Household effects of Mrs Cook,** widow of the Circumnavigator. Perhaps the tray with china, on top of the small chest of drawers, was from the cabin of one of Cook's ships.

Death as the end of a voyage of exploration also broods over another famous group of relics in the Museum. From the ice-bound Arctic regions of North America, the remaining battered possessions of members of Sir John Franklin's 1845 expedition in search of the North-West Passage to the Pacific were recovered and sent to Greenwich Hospital as memorials to endurance and frustrated hopes. There were no survivors and it was 1854 before the fate of the crews of HM Ships *Erebus* and *Terror* was established; the passage of time heightened public concern and interest in the relics.

**Curiosities from Captain Cook's voyages.** On a background of native *tapa* cloth are (*from left*) a stone breadfruit pounder or *poi* from Tahiti; head of a *tewhatewha* from New Zealand; carved head of a club from Tonga; a Maori club or *patu*; and a wooden 'seal' bowl from the Canadian N.W. coast.

**Death in Victory.** Lord Nelson's undress coat worn at Trafalgar shows the hole in the left shoulder from the musket shot that killed him. The stars of the Orders of Knighthood, which he always wore, are the Bath (*top*), St. Ferdinand and of Merit (*below left*), the Crescent (*below right*) and St. Joachim (*bottom*).

**Captain Sir John Franklin,** portrait flanked by relics of his lost 1845 Arctic Expedition, found by searchers: his Hanoverian Guelphic Order, silver spoons with officers' initials and crests, blades, buttons, a piece of flannel with a laundry mark, a Royal Marine shako plate and the remains of a pocket watch.

## Sculpture

The distinguished officers guarding two of the Museum's entrances stood originally in the Painted Hall of Greenwich Hospital. They gesture grandly, marble swords sheathed, buckled shoes and boots planted on decks and on coils of marble rope. Lord Exmouth, Sir Sidney Smith, Sir William Peel and Lord de Saumarez are modelled larger than life, and their exploits are part of British history. Their comrades and predecessors are immortalized inside the Museum in busts of bronze, stone, wood, terracotta and plaster, in their places along the galleries among the painted scenes of their actions. Admiral Vernon, the turbulent, humane officer who was also a Member of Parliament and a writer is depicted.

**Keppel's Head and other Admirals.** A relief in vitreous paste by Tassie, of Augustus Viscount Keppel (*centre*), flanked by Wedgwood jasper heads of Lord Howe (*left*), Lord Nelson (*right*), Lord Duncan (*above left*), and Lord St. Vincent (*above right*). Framed in contemporary style, Lord Duncan by Tassie (*below left*) and Sir William Hamilton, husband of Emma (*right*), by Wedgwood.

Nelson is shown in several poses, whilst Sir Walter Raleigh, the American John Paul Jones, the Scot Adam Duncan and the Italian astronomer Galileo, as well as distinguished officers from the Victorian age, are set in their places. The heads of leaders of the Second World War, commissioned by Government as reminders of the men who carried on a great tradition, are also present: Sir Philip Vian, Sir William James and Sir Charles Little. Portrait busts of Richard Green, shipowner and philanthropist of the nearby Blackwall shipyard, and of Joseph Allen, a minor figure who lost both legs in action, held an appointment in Greenwich Hospital and became an author, contrast with that of the child Horatia, Nelson's daughter by Emma, Lady Hamilton. Wax portraits of famous officers of Georgian times including one of a little-known captain, Richard Gwynn, seated at his table, are further evidence of the ever-fashionable desire for remembrance.

**Ships on Glasses** for toasting success in war and trade as well as glorious memory. (*From left*): Nelson's funeral procession, 1806; Newcastle *c* 1750 Dutch-engraved *Vivat Negosiae*; goblet with silver coin in hollow stem showing brig sailing under Sunderland Bridge, 1830; large goblet inscribed *Captain S. B. Dunn 1856*; the capture of Havannah in 1762 by the brothers General Lord Albemarle and Admiral Augustus Keppel, engraved with a toast; the brig *William* of London, 1809.

**Horatio Nelson,** sculpted by Lawrence Gahagan in terra cotta, *c* 1801.

The Queen's House from the north-west.